SELF-EMPLOY

Also available from Cassell:

Evans: *Supervisory Management*, 5th edition

Forsyth: *Career Skills*

Goddard: *Informative Writing*, 2nd edition

Mendelsohn: *The Guide to Franchising*, 6th edition

Maitland: *The Small Business Marketing Handbook*

Pettinger: *Managing the Flexible Workforce*

Walker, Ferguson and Denvir: *Creating New Clients*

Self-Employment

Making It Work for You

**John Spencer
and Adrian Pruss**

CASSELL

Cassell

Wellington House
125 Strand
London WC2R 0BB

370 Lexington Avenue
New York
NY 10017-6550

First published 2000

British Library Cataloguing-in-Publication Data
A catalogue record for this book is available from the British Library.

ISBN 0-304-70501-2

Typeset by ensystems Ltd, Saffron Walden, Essex
Printed in Great Britain by Biddles Ltd, Guildford and King's Lynn

Contents

Acknowledgements

Our GRATEFUL THANKS to: David Cooper, Small Business Manager of Barclays Bank Hatton Garden; Jez Rodrigo, Business Manager of Barclays Bank St Albans Group; Dennis Gowans of BP Amoco; Howard Thompson, and Chris Heaton-Armstrong, who variously provided us with advice, information and invaluable comments on certain specialist chapters.

Our especial thanks also to the many interviewees who contributed, particularly Martin Attridge, John Badeker, Ivan Berg, Onay Faiz, Jim and Breda Fortune, Sarah Francis, Richard Grossman, Kirsten Klingels, Andrew Leigh, Mike Maynard, Tony Player, Bob Rontaler, James Wildman, and Gerry Zierler, and also to the many who gave interviews but preferred to remain anonymous, and to the thousands of clients whose experiences have provided a rich source of material.

Introduction

THERE ARE ESTIMATED to be 3.3 million self-employed people in the UK at the present time. The number is likely to grow, given the tendency of companies to outsource work to independents, and engage people on temporary assignments rather than long-term employment contracts.

This book is a companion and a reference work for all of them. It offers both the experiences of the self-employed through quoted interviews, and the practicalities of 'how to do it' based on the work of its two authors.

The authors are a chartered accountant and a management consultant who, between them, have over 50 years' experience with businesses of all sizes and types across the whole spectrum of industry and commerce. John Spencer is managing partner of Connor, Spencer & Co., Chartered Accountants, which specializes in the development of small businesses and has acted for thousands of clients in that capacity. Adrian Pruss is a City-trained accountant and management consultant specializing in organizational review, cost reduction, and change programmes, and has worked in several countries.

In addition to their direct knowledge and experience they draw from thousands of 'client hours' of experience – many gave direct interviews for this book – to put together a definitive handbook about what self-employment really means, with its ups and downs, and its effect on home life, relationships and personal organization.

Although the self-employed are often bracketed into one category, Chapter 1 explains the diverse routes through which people come to that status, and the differences are important to understand in order that each reader can appreciate his or her particular situation.

The book is also based on the countless questions that self-employed and would-be self-employed ask when setting out on that road. Both authors have spent years collating those questions, and this book gives the answers.

The recent introduction of self-assessment has probably created more changes to the world of the self-employed than any other recent legislation, and it has created fear and misunderstanding. The authors have direct experience of dealing with compliance and investigation under self-assessment since its inception: indeed they were preparing for self-assessment for two years prior to its introduction.

Reading this book gives the self-employed a route-map of how to succeed and a far better chance of survival in a very aggressive, and always exciting, environment.

1 / The Routes to Self-Employment

SELF-EMPLOYMENT IS literally a state of mind and a way of life, not just a way of working. People become self-employed through a variety of routes and for a number of reasons, and, while everyone has the potential to succeed, the most successful are those who understand the differences and understand how they chose the path they are on.

We have identified the following as the most common backgrounds to self-employment.

Family culture

There is every evidence that children role-model their parents. Children of self-employed parents are more likely to go into self-employment in some form than those of employee-parents. Similarly, the children of employee-parents usually follow their parents, if not into the same jobs, then into the same culture, i.e. employment rather than self-employment.

There are probably several factors which determine this:

First, those who have grown up in households where the parents are self-employed have seen that it can be a success, and their barriers to risk are lower than those with employee-parents for whom the basic fear of self-employment is usually expressed as lack of job security. They are used to the fact that earnings can be erratic, but they have seen that the potential can be for higher income overall.

Second, they will have seen the reverse side of the 'job security' logic. For a self-employed person with 500 clients it takes 500 people to 'sack' him or her; the employee can be sacked by a single person. Since there are no longer any 'jobs for life', job security now lies not in employment but in the diversity and range of skill-applications and the numbers of clients and customers of the self-employed.

Third, they are used to the flexibility of working hours which is a feature of self-employment and they see its advantages. The ability to take time off without pre-warning when needed (balanced by the need to often work longer hours) is attractive. It is a practical application of having control over their own lives, a very real desire for most people.

Following on from the 'control of your own life' is the 'be your own boss' culture. Children of self-employed parents grow up in an atmosphere of self-determination and the 'maverick' culture of 'doing things your own way'. It is hard to be a good employee coming from that culture, not least because 'toeing the company line' and doing things according to the company rule book is often frustrating.

One client we interviewed, John Badeker, told us:

I always intended to be self-employed but I figured it was wise to do an 'apprenticeship' in a firm for a number of years as an employee to get to 'know the ropes'. So I did. But it was a hard time. I was constantly bucking up against my bosses. I knew – or at least I thought I knew – the best ways to get things done and I wanted to do them my way, but I was constantly being criticized for not sticking to the tried and tested procedures. But what they realized was that their tried and tested procedures didn't produce anything like the results I did, and they were torn between wanting me to obey the rules and keeping up my productivity. I was the only section manager in five years who had turned in a profit in that department, a service department within the company. They had to acknowledge that but it came hard to them. I think, in fact, that it eventually would have been a stumbling block to my promotion; I was rubbing a lot of people up the wrong way. But it didn't matter. When I was ready I got out. Now I run my own business. It's a lot smaller than the company I used to work for, but pound for pound of investment it's a hell of a lot more profitable. And I'm a sight happier now than I was then. I can do things my way now; and I love it.

The fact that a large number of the self-employed become so through the 'family culture' demonstrates also that self-employment is not just a way of working, it is a way of life. Families – family time, family finances, family attitudes – are based around the circumstances of self-employment, and it becomes a natural way of life for children to follow up in their own later lives.

Accountants can usually tell those new clients that come from such backgrounds. Their questions at initial interviews are based around the business they will be working in retail, printing, etc. – and not around the mechanics of self-employment. They don't need to ask about paying tax to the Inland Revenue, paying their own National Insurance contributions, understanding VAT, and so on. They've heard all that around the breakfast table all their lives! Such people are successful because many of the states of mind and attitudes that are needed to become self-employed are already learned; indeed almost inbred. With the 'mechanics' out of the way, they can get on with running their businesses and making profits.

Farming culture

This is not literally restricted to farming, but a culture that first developed in rural practices in earlier times. Put simply, it is expected that the eldest son will follow the father into his business. In more modern times the gender barriers are largely down and we see daughters following fathers or mothers into the 'family business', but the principle is unchanged.

What is significant is that although such people have all the advantages of the 'family culture' mentioned above, they suffer from one drawback – a perceived lack of choice. They are *expected* to take over from the parents, and they know it from an early age. Many love that security, many are successful. But some go into the business with reluctance, and perhaps a lack of real drive. Perhaps they, too, pass on that lack of drive or ability while passing on the attitudes of the 'family culture' – it is said that the first generation starts the business, the second generation grows it, and the third generation destroys it. We have certainly seen examples of this. By the third generation the up-and-coming business owners have often been seduced into the way of life of self-employment, making them virtually unemployable in any other work culture, but they do not have the 'breath of the poorhouse on their necks' to motivate them. However, they do have a belief that this business that has been around all their lives and before must be permanent and impossible to lose. Many later find that latter assumption wrong!

The expectation that they will follow the parents into the business is demonstrated in many ways. Children will be involved in simple decisions of the business from quite an early age; they will sit in on discussions around the house about the business; they will tend to work in that business during weekends and holidays while others get paper-rounds and jobs in shops. As they get older the assumption that they will follow their parents becomes taken for granted, until the children feel they have little choice in the matter.

A further disadvantage of the 'farming culture' is the complacency that goes with the knowledge from formative years onwards that there is a job waiting to be plucked off the tree. There will be no need to ever attend an interview, no need to think of yourself as a commodity that must be sold to a potential employer or even client, no need to take risks. All that has been done for you. The lack of threat or stress in this circumstance can lead to a high level of complacency. For some it rids them of unwanted problems and allows them to move faster into the business; for others it takes away their edge.

Those who become self-employed through this route have many advantages – all of the advantages of the 'family culture' in particular – and they are often very successful, so these caveats are not to be regarded as hurdles that cannot be overcome.

Many of the disadvantages that come with the 'farming culture' are conquered by training. The basic awarenesses of self-employment are there, but it is the interpersonal skills that are needed: communication skills, consideration of the needs of others, and so on.

Redundancy

There is an increasing tendency for people to become self-employed as a result of being made redundant, or accepting voluntary redundancy. For example, BT had a round of large-scale redundancies as part of their programme Streamline 2000, which resulted in a large number of people leaving their employment with generous packages, some of around £50,000. Some came to the decision as a result of finding that they were no longer employable, often regarded as too old. Others chose to take the opportunity presented to start a small business, often fulfilling an ambition.

Many people taking this route find that they do not have the essential qualities of self-employment, not having grown up in such a culture and perhaps not feeling that it is inherently 'right' for them. Some are actually apprehensive when they start, and a certain boldness and risk-taking is a requirement of success.

Their motivations are also different. They are not seeking to build a business which will give them a certain standard of living, nor make a significant contribution to the world through their own vision of a business. Rather, they are often marking time to their retirement, or making a relatively desperate move to earn a living in the only way they see open to them. Either way their expectations and motivations are lower, and their chances – and degrees – of success are correspondingly lower.

But these deficiencies can be eliminated. The question of limited aims is not one for correction as it is largely a matter of choice, though many find that with their attitudes changed their expectations increase. But basic training of the 'territory' of self-employment, attempting to put the traditions of the 'family culture' in place by learning, can make a great difference. Such people will benefit greatly from this book; it provides a map of the territory into which they are about to venture.

What such people need mostly is an awareness of the financial implications of self-employment: no regular income and a need to budget for taxation, VAT, and a reserve for times when money is not flowing as at other times. Budgeting becomes an essential way of life, and the techniques of business budgeting are an essential tool.

Before such people decide whether or not to take a self-employed route they should also ask themselves if they are the 'self-starters' that such work requires. Self-employed people do not have to be asked or told to start work – they should be itching to start work. As one commented:

I thought, on becoming self-employed, that I might have trouble going to my desk in the morning. I feared I would distract myself in a whole host of ways, and that I might waste large chunks of the day that way. But in fact my wife tells me that the problem is not getting me to my desk, it's getting me away from it. Frequently I find I need, or want, to stay at my desk until midnight. But I don't mind; I'm working for me now.

Such people must also ask if they can work alone. Many who took employment as their natural route did so, knowingly or unknowingly, because they liked working in groups with others, and liked the 'buzz' of people around them. The self-employed are often in isolation. As one person joked: 'Self-employment's great; but the office parties are a bit dull!'

For those who fit the criteria, being forced into self-employment can be the best move they ever made, and we have often heard the cry 'if only I'd done this sooner'. But there is a body of people for whom self-employment becomes the latest in a long line of disasters: the redundancy package is eaten away and the need to find some sort of job, often more lowly paid than the previous employment, becomes the only way out. The best that many such people can say is 'I'm glad I tried, but never again!'

Many large companies offer redundancy assistance to those who are made redundant or who volunteer for redundancy. For example, they pay for training in new skills such as IT, they assist in writing CVs for their former employees, and so on.

Redundancy and reinstatement

Almost a sub-set of the group above are those people who are forced into self-employment by redundancy but who in effect never actually change their jobs.

Many large companies have instigated policies of outsourcing, and of moving to contractors rather than employees. In many cases people are offered voluntary redundancies but are then given self-employed contracts to continue doing the same work. In effect they pick up their £50,000 and their P45 on the Friday, then go back to the same desk on the Monday and continue as before, but now officially self-employed.

The advantage of such an arrangement for the employer is that they are freed from the commitments of holiday pay, pay when there is no work, and other fixed costs such as pensions, insurances, and supplying benefit packages such as cars and medical health cover. They are also freed from the bureaucracy of the PAYE system of tax deduction. For the 'employee', now contractor, the advantage is that contractors are generally paid a higher rate for the hours they do work, and at least in theory they are free to take on other work when their former employers do not require their services.

Some such contractors in fact never work for anyone else, and continue virtually as they did. Others treat the contract with their former employers as a stepping stone to building a true consultancy, taking on other clients. The latter are 'more' self-employed at least in their outlook. But their greatest danger is that they set up their own business infrastructure – loans, equipment, and so on – on the basis of the one big contract and either fail to find other such contracts or indeed 'rest on their laurels' and almost immediately collapse as a business when that contract comes to an end. Most such people find they have a lack of marketing expertise – they fail either to sell themselves adequately, or indeed to realize that they must now do so. Marketing and self-promotion become very important attributes to acquire for such people.

Those who choose to take this route should always be seeking to negotiate the right to work for other companies, and they should immediately be actively seeking future contracts. It is never too late to start winning, as the old adage says.

They are helped in this by Inland Revenue rules which can deem a person to be an employee whatever the engaging company would like to claim (such rules are covered in a later chapter). However, some outsourcing bypasses these Inland Revenue rules by either using agencies – the former employee is directed to an agency which employs them and then subcontracts them back to the original company – or by forcing the former employee to set up a Limited Company through which to trade, which is then acceptable to the Inland Revenue. (The Inland Revenue is seeking to restrict the 'Limited Company' route; it has recently released IR35, setting out such intentions.) The 'agency' option is usually agreeable to those former employees who recognize that they do not wish to be truly self-employed; they are in effect switching employers, although perhaps with less job security than they previously had. The latter route is probably more acceptable to those who are ready to try to make a 'go' of their own business. With the removal of onerous regulations relating to limited companies (also covered in a later chapter), this is an increasingly attractive proposition for people who find themselves self-employed in these circumstances.

Shortage of employment

For some who are made redundant or otherwise find themselves out of work the option to continue in their previously chosen line of work does not exist, or they find it difficult to accomplish. There is therefore a further division of people who find themselves self-employed, who discover that in addition to grappling with the complexities of the self-employed culture they also have to learn new trades.

For example, many factory workers that have been replaced by changing technologies find their skill-base redundant. Furthermore, sometimes a whole town or area of the country, can be devastated by a major employer shutting down or transferring to another area or country leaving a sudden and huge pool of unemployed people in an area with few jobs. In those circumstances a few lucky ones – the best of the pool – might find work but many are forced to find alternatives. Factory workers might turn their hand to the building trade, or become 'jobbing decorators', or self-employed mini-cab drivers, or a range of other skills for which a long period of training is not required.

Such people, often of the older generation, are too proud to 'sign on' as unemployed and take state benefits, and they often end up working for little or no profit. Good business advice from an accountant can assist such people in recognizing the opportunities that are presented and in some cases can create bigger and more 'serious' businesses than might otherwise have developed, to the obvious advantage of the newly self-employed individual. Sometimes this is just a change of perspective; such people often take the view that their purpose is to 'make a living' rather than 'create a business'. Those who accept the latter path usually end up far better off financially.

Such people are usually so concerned to get themselves into work and begin earning that they find themselves dealing with day-to-day needs while ignoring their legal requirements to notify the Inland Revenue, Contributions Agency and VAT office of their new status, an omission which results in fines, penalties and punitive investigations. While it is difficult to see how those official bodies could operate without penalties to bring such people 'into the net' it is troubling that these people, often the most innocent and confused of those who find themselves self-employed, face such penalties when what they really need is support. The fact that the new tax regime recently introduced has reduced the notification time to six months after the end of the tax year in which the trade starts (it used to be one year) has only made matters worse.

People becoming self-employed are advised to seek out the services of an accountant who can advise them, and to do so as soon as possible after the decision to commence has been taken. This group more than any needs to do just that. Accountants are skilled at taking the bureaucracy away from the individual and making all the necessary notifications. They can also advise on many other important aspects, as set out in a later chapter. The individual is then free to get on with establishing and building his or her business.

The publican culture

Some people come to self-employment as a product of finding their own natural flair and desire through working in relatively unskilled work. The archetype of this, which gives the 'publican culture' its name, is the bar-hand who works in the pub, perhaps serving, or washing up, or preparing the food, who learns the trade and eventually buys his or her own pub, or takes a tenancy.

In Chapter 6 Jim Fortune discusses his attitude to his self-employment in just such circumstances.

Such people perhaps always have the necessary spark about them, indeed in some ways they may be the most natural of the self-employed group with all the talents, confidence and drive needed. But not coming from a 'family culture' of self-employment they have no background and therefore tend to come to self-employment later in life through the route of watching and waiting in their employment.

A version of this 'publican culture' is where a member of staff marries the owner or licensee and becomes part of the business through that route, often showing their entrepreneurial flair and business abilities.

Typically businesses of this nature would include, apart from pubs, small building companies, restaurants, mini-cabs and printing firms.

Fulfilling an ambition

Some people come to self-employment late in life. They may have been happy in their jobs throughout their lives (some of course may not have been), but around the age of 45 to 55 they realize that one ambition they have had is to be their own boss.

Their motivations, and their goals for their businesses, are quite different from many that we have looked at above. They do not seek to grow large businesses, nor indeed to create lucrative incomes; their motivation is not 'to be self-employed' but very much, as stated, 'to be their own boss'. Their motivation is to use their creative talents which have perhaps remained suppressed in their jobs, and to have a measure of the independence which self-employment brings.

They are not risk-takers. The reason they choose self-employment late in life is because they wait until the mortgage is paid or, having remained in the same house for some decades, they have a relatively small mortgage depleted as much by inflation as repayment. Their children have grown up and left home. They have also come to realize that the job they hold now is largely the job they will hold until retirement; they have virtually reached the end of their career path. So they have the opportunity presented by low-income needs, and they take it.

But in order to find a niche for themselves they tend to look for work that interests them rather than work that is lucrative. They often turn their hobbies into businesses and many go into publishing, writing, or activities associated with computers. Many have followed those paths as hobbies, a few might have made a few pounds doing such services 'on the side' for friends and relatives. And when they make the break from work they turn the business into an extension of their old hobby. They are not great marketing people, preferring to work at a low ebb, based on word-of-mouth promotion, and making enough only to cover a low-income lifestyle.

Many such people are loners, some of whom feel they have never had much opportunity to indulge that need – to be with themselves. Employment can be a way of working that allows for very little isolation, particularly with the modern trend for corporate teams, and while that suits many people it can be frustrating for some. For those people this move is an opportunity to enjoy their solitude.

For many this is a very suitable path towards retirement; it is virtually a semi-retirement paying the bills along the way. They build in a large amount of free time, time on the golf course, and so on. To some extent they kid themselves that they play golf, or other social activities, as part of their business promotion but in fact they do not. If they could fill every day with work they would run a mile; that is not their true ambition. Indeed, we have seen a few people who have chosen this path who either by luck or natural talent revealed too late have created very successful businesses; and they either neglect them or in extreme cases become their own saboteurs, damaging their own businesses. From their point of view it seems that they cannot cope with the pressures. From an accountant's point of view they are not particularly pressured, and these businesses virtually run themselves sometimes, but still the proprietors turn away good work, fail to take up leads, and so on, and it is very clear that they simply do not want the business to take that path, to engage in that level of activity.

'Normal' social pressures seem to force people to always 'make the most' of opportunities, and see lost opportunities as a sinful waste. This is nonsense. People must carve out their own paths, and once these people come to terms with their own inner motivations they – and their friends and relatives – are much more contented.

The one big mistake that we have seen such people make is to be seduced towards franchising as a route to self-employment. Franchising is discussed in a later chapter, but suffice it to say here that the upfront costs and the pressures from most franchisors is such that you have to enter that kind of business with a view to it being full-time. Franchises do not pay for themselves at the part-time level, and people who want a 'path to retirement' find franchising a waste of their time and money, as well as highly pressured and frustrating.

Getting off the treadmill

Call it the hamsters' treadmill, or the rat race, or just the 8.30 a.m. marathon walk over Waterloo Bridge, but by whatever name, for some the pressures of a high-powered job nine-to-five, possibly in a sprawling city centre like London, get to be too much. People suffer burn-out, stress, lack of direction or whatever, and they simply do not want to work in those jobs any more.

They start to talk about the quality of life, of wanting to have more time with children or more time at home. In our experience as consultants in large corporations when someone mentions those topics, they're gone in six months!

Some, perhaps having put a nest-egg away, leave their jobs and are happy to engage in work lacking pressure. We know of one city executive who now works four days a week serving in his local shop in the village from where he commuted for 30 years. But for others the exit route off the treadmill is through self-employment.

Self-employment can take many forms: simple work like gardening and decorating; sometimes a slowed-down version of the previous employment, perhaps a consultancy in the same field working just a few days a week; perhaps they take the 'hobby' route similar to that mentioned under 'Fulfilling an ambition' above. For others it is the pressure and lifestyle rather than the hours that matter, and they choose to buy and run a pub or a shop. Anyone who thinks that either of these is a 'soft option' is wrong; they both involve long hours and a considerable investment of concentration. But for escapees from the 'rat race' the change of pressure from one type to another, the pressures of being 'your own boss' as opposed to being at the beck and call of bosses, committees and powerful clients, can be a refreshing one.

The policeman and fireman culture

Two routes to self-employment are embodied by the 'policeman and fireman culture'. The nature of their employment virtually forces them into retirement after 20 years, while still relatively young. Many large companies, including those in the financial services sector and petro-chemical industries, are retiring staff early. Being 'retired' at around 40 to 45 years old allows some of these people to take self-employment as a route forwards. They capitalize on their skills and expertise and start consultancies in their own fields. For example, policemen might start security firms, firemen start fire safety or health and safety consultancies.

Often, in the run-up to becoming self-employed, such individuals run their own consultancies in tandem with their employments. The hours demanded of, say, firemen, involve long periods of inactivity or being on call, but at home, which allows for a 'secondary' business. These businesses then become the basis of a more full-time consultancy when they retire from their employments. It must be said that in many cases such activities are either directly opposed to the terms of their employment contracts, or are indeed illegal given the requirement to be fit and alert during work-times; nonetheless there are many such situations. As accountants we have often been asked to ensure that the Inland Revenue fulfils its obligations of confidentiality by not revealing the self-employment to existing employers.

The MD of a large electrical wholesalers in the south-east of England, whom we interviewed, started his business while selling his own products from his bosses' van, and has now built an £8 million-plus business with its own proprietary brands.

Government contracts

There are some self-employed people who, by virtue of the nature of their profession, are virtually only semi-self-employed in that they have substantial government contracts underpinning their businesses. For example, doctors who run their own practices have income from the National Health Service. They are legally self-employed and must obey all the rules of self-employment but we refer to them as semi-self-employed to take into account the fact that they do not have to greatly concern themselves with some aspects of self-employment such as aggressive marketing, some financial planning (given that they have regular income from their contracts), and so on.

New Age practices

There is a whole raft of self-employed based on what might be called the 'New Age'. These are the alternative and complementary healing and counselling practices that include yoga, dance therapy, meditation, t'ai chi, diet, herbal medicines and homeopathy, hypnotherapy, crystal healing, reflexology, acupuncture, acupressure, shiatsu, massage, aromatherapy, rebirthing and vivation, reiki therapy, and so on *ad infinitum*.

We have many such clients who run such businesses on profitable, professional lines. They are often escapees from the caring professions such as nursing, counselling, and so on. The majority of such businesses are run by women, who take the self-employed route for various reasons, the three main ones being:

a) rejection of what they see as the restricted viewpoints towards healing of the NHS,
b) a chance to improve their income, and
c) an opportunity to control their lifestyles better, combining work and home life, and perhaps child-rearing, to their better advantage.

But in addition to these professional practitioners are a substantial number who are in many ways well-meaning amateurs as far as business goes. They are often the domestic partners of well-heeled and successful individuals. Some are independently wealthy people, some divorcees with large settlements. In fact they usually make little or no profit. They are – there is no more polite term for it – *playing* at being self-employed. Their motivations are quite different from almost any other. Their businesses are virtually trophies and talking points rather than serious enterprises. This should not be taken as criticism of them or their chosen work – they would argue that they are using their businesses to put back into the community some of their wealth – but our point is only that such an outlook does not fit into the general pattern of attitudes towards self-employment. Their counterparts in employment would be those who give their time freely, or at low cost, to charity organizations.

Having specialist expertise

Some experts in their field can command very high fees for their work. Self-employment becomes a good way for them to manage their lives, particularly as in addition to the advantages of self-employment such as freedom to work or not work certain hours, the divide between the rates of pay for salaried or self-employed can be very high. Highly paid specialists going self-employed might increase their earnings potential threefold just by changing to running their own business.

The newest entries to this market are filling skills shortages in large companies that arise for three main reasons: peak lopping, i.e. the practice of taking on experts to accommodate a perceived short-term increase in activity; gaps existing until suitable full-time employees can be found; and third, shortages caused by lack of training particularly in companies that withdrew training as a cost-saving measure.

The Millennium Bug is the latest such 'specialist area'. We know of one consultant who was earning £36,000 per annum and who now commands £2000 per day to assist large companies in dealing with 'The Bug' problems.

Being a polymath

Some people seem to require a greater variety of occupations than others, and such people are constrained within 'conventional' jobs where, for the most part, job demarcation is the norm. In former decades most such people rarely found outlets for these needs in work, channelling their desires into their hobbies. Nowadays they can either turn their hobbies into part of their self-employment – computer enthusiasts making part of their living from computer consultancy for example – or channel their need for variety into several areas of self-employment simultaneously.

The authors of this book, for example, have a variety of activities all of which are valid areas of profitable business. John Spencer is an author of business books, an author of science fiction and paranormal books, a management trainer and consultant, and a chartered accountant with his own practice. Adrian Pruss is a management consultant and trainer, a chartered secretary, director of several diverse companies, and co-author with John Spencer of several business books. We also work with one management training company which draws from the arts and entertainment world where, for example, one trainer lists his specialities as computer consultant and trained fire-eater!

To be successful in these ways requires certain clear talents, such as time and diary management, and an ability to dislocate the thinking of one form of work from that of the others.

The possible downside is the danger of becoming a jack of all trades and a master of none; the upside is not only in the variety of challenges but in the fresh approaches that can be brought to each area of work by drawing from the skills of other areas.

2

Learning from Those Who Have Gone Before You: Thoughts of the Self-Employed

WHAT IS IT actually like to wake up each day as your own boss?

It is not like waking up as an employee. While it is important to put aside the business sometimes and have a personal life, one defining feature of self-employment is that when you wake up at four o'clock in the morning the business is often the thing most on your mind. When you read an article in a newspaper some part of your mind is thinking 'how can I make that work for me in my business?'

We interviewed several self-employed people and asked them to explain what, for them, had been the most important aspects of that way of life. Their answers have been collated into this chapter.

Relationships

We asked about relationships within the family. How had self-employment affected spouse and children, friends and other family?

Martin Attridge, a training and development consultant:
At first it was relatively easy. I was contracted to the company I had been working for, so it was a relatively smooth transition. So it was not a huge difference as far as the children or family were concerned, nor in terms of social life, at first. I guess the more dramatic changes have come over the last couple of years where I have been running three- or four-day courses and spending a lot of time away

from home as a result. Leaving Monday and coming back on a Friday night at often late times means the weekend is necessarily compacted. I'm just not there during the week for the family at all.

My wife has been able to cope with the children, but I think she probably misses company in the evenings, and perhaps has sought to go out more with friends as a result simply to get the social contact. I think that makes the weekends quite difficult as well because often the last thing I normally want to do at the weekend is go out but of course both my wife and children do want to. I think there is some conflict there which needs to be talked through and it's not necessarily easily resolvable.

My children are quite old now and independent so it's probably not as much of a problem as it would have been, say, five years ago or so. I think I would have had to have made a very tough decision about whether I was prepared to go away if the children had been between, say, seven and twelve, something like that.

The children have taken the change of lifestyle quite well. They are used to see me home every weekend. Of course when I do come home I get dumped on. Not always bad stuff but in a sense everything that's been going on that particular week or their problems. I think they've got used to it now and as long as they see me every weekend they are not too bothered. But if they had been younger I think it would have been much more difficult to sustain.

Onay Faiz of Phoenix Training Network – management training services:
Unfortunately, I would say that self-employment had a few negative effects on my relationship with my partner of seven years. Because I set up my office from our shared home, in the second of our two bedrooms, my partner felt a bit aggrieved that 'my stuff' took over the bedroom. I'd set up office in the spare bedroom which had previously been his 'playroom'; he would play on his computer for hours, read, make models and do boys' stuff. I don't know quite how this transpired when we'd bought the house, but he got the 'playroom' and I got the kitchen!

The 'space' thing did became a bit of an issue. A business

takes up a fair bit of space when you run it from home – especially a small 2-bedroom house. I recall single-handedly stuffing 20,000 A4-sized brochures into 20,000 envelopes in my lounge. That's a lot of paper, and it meant I took over yet another room with tottering towers of envelope bundles for about eight days. He was pretty upset about that.

Somehow, I always had the feeling that my partner was less proud of me because I worked from home. Once the glamour of my working in publishing as a magazine editor, travelling the country and sometimes the world, was gone (as I started up my own business), my partner seemed a bit disappointed. Maybe it removed a bit of the mystery in our relationship, the mystery of what I did at work all day when I was employed, the people I knew and the responsibilities I held. Perhaps that all seemed more intangible and exciting to him than seeing me tapping away at the computer in the bedroom at home all day. I guess 'My girlfriend's in Chicago' is much more impressive than 'My girlfriend works from home'.

For me it was great, though. Working alone at home, I found I could very successfully plan my jobs for the day and motor through them at a good pace without the interruptions that an office environment brings. In publishing, the phone constantly rings, people constantly interrupt, and it's very difficult to concentrate on a major task. Interruptions meant I would spend much more time getting through a single day's workload, often having to catch up in the evenings once it had quietened down a bit. At home, my time management and ability to get things finished improved tremendously. Consequently, I could happily work a 9–5.30 day, and be downstairs relaxing at 5.35 p.m.

The only problem with this was that my partner would come home at 7.30 p.m., or some such time, to find me well engrossed in my evening's activities, whether it was cooking, playing my piano, ironing, catching up on a weekly soap, reading, or whatever. Coupled with the fact that he always left for London very early in the mornings, while I'd still be in my pyjamas having a not-too-early leisurely start to the day, I had the feeling that he rather assumed I went from pyjamas to TV and did little else in between. I guess that's because he rarely saw me working, or leaving for an appointment in my business togs. It did set a strange kind of view in his mind.

No more was I coming home late, or long after he'd got in. I believe he felt I didn't work very hard simply because I wasn't having to put mammoth hours in. My view is: I didn't go self-employed to work late evenings and weekends like I had done with the publishing company. I wanted a job I could enjoy and work hard at, but which didn't take over my life.

There does seem to be a bit of a stigma attached to people working from home; the idea that they're on a cushy number, making cups of tea and watching soaps on telly all day. I sometimes picked up this attitude from friends and neighbours. They'd ask, 'But don't you want to just pop downstairs and finish off that washing up during the day?' The answer is easy: No. I had no problem sticking to my office hours.

I also found that neighbours would drop in for a chat at any time, so I had to get the message across that I was working all day by keeping the interruptions short and sweet – and on the doorstep – or else invite them back 'after work'. The message got across, and people respected it.

Regarding how self-employment affected my family, I have no family members here in Britain. Consequently, I was a bit nervous of going into self-employment. If it all failed miserably, I had no safety net to fall in. That was scary, I suppose. As for relationships with friends, I found that it didn't affect my relationships with them greatly.

Tony Player of WHS Fabrications, one of the top construction companies in the 'second division' of its field, with a turnover of between £5 and £6 million:
Self-employment is a lot more difficult to deal with than direct employment purely on the basis that you are with the job 100 per cent of the time. You never really leave it behind. The people I employ go home and then strictly speaking they don't have to think about the job until the following day. Plus they go on holiday for two weeks, three weeks and they forget about it. I never forget it. It's always in the back of my mind. But I think self-employment is great.

With self-employment it's the personal burden that you have to bear but you have to learn not to take too much of it home with you otherwise it does start to affect your personal life. In fact I don't want to talk about work when I get home. I find I go home and listen more than I talk.

Mike Maynard and *Andrew Leigh* are the original partners of Maynard Leigh Associates, a £million-plus training and consultancy organization:
Mike: I feel totally responsible now in a way I never did when I was just freelancing. I just felt something in those days to the family, me and my family. And now I feel for the staff and associates here; their employment is my responsibility.

Financial uncertainty

We asked about how the uncertainty of finances resulting from self-employment had affected personal life, and whether it was regarded as more insecure.

James Wildman of Wild Communications – editorial, marketing and PR, print and design services:
When I first became self-employed I was single and living at home and the only real impact was having to work on my own and feeling cut off from the outside world. I then met someone through work who became my girlfriend and later my wife. The fact I was self-employed was a big issue between us, mostly negative, as she had been in the same job since leaving school and found the uncertainty difficult to deal with. She wanted to have regular holidays and couldn't grasp the concept of not knowing how much money on a month-to-month basis I was earning.

I managed to overcome my own financial insecurity by always giving myself a three-month cushion – having enough money put aside so that if I had no work for three months I could still live.

Onay Faiz:
Yes, I was very concerned about the financial security aspect. The reason is that my family doesn't reside in this

country and, therefore, I was very much on my own, with no safe haven to fall back on. If I lost my home as a result of the business not sustaining itself, I couldn't fall back on living with mum and dad for a while. That made me pretty nervous.

My partner and I – now ex-partner – were not living as a financially supporting couple. Though we shared a house, we split everything 50:50 and so I could not rely on him for any real financial rescue if things didn't work out. Before I started up, I asked him to support me by paying my half of the mortgage for the first few months if I was struggling. He reluctantly agreed. It never became necessary, thank goodness.

Has it affected my outlook? Yes, I guess so. I found a lot of things were harder to achieve if you were self-employed – mortgages, loans, endowments, credit facilities. It would sometimes annoy me that self-employment seemed to be a dirty word in financial circles. But once I'd reached my third year, things looked better with a track record of accounts.

I had a huge panic in 1998 when my partner and I split up. I wanted to buy his share of the house off him yet found I had major problems securing a mortgage because my business hadn't shown enough profit in its first few years. It seemed there were shut doors everywhere. Nobody wanted to help, and I could see myself homeless, having to go back to employment as well as giving up my business because I simply couldn't operate it from a home I didn't have. That was quite frightening, and I realized that you benefit so much from having the safety net support from a partner or family, even if they're simply paying half the bills in your home and sharing life's costs with you.

I was lucky enough to find a good financial advisor who discovered a mortgage company that specializes in offering self-employed people home loans.

One of the biggest mistakes I made, once I went self-employed, was spending at the same level I was used to when I was employed. When you start up, you have to be much more careful with your money and expenses; earnings are unlikely to be at the same level during the start-up period.

Martin Attridge:
My wife has a full time, well-paid job. If she hadn't I would have been a lot more circumspect about self-employment. On the other hand I think if she hadn't had a job maybe I would have thought a lot harder in terms of winning and doing business. As a self-criticism, I think I've been a little bit too complacent knowing that the money is not the be-all and end-all and there has not been a real necessity to work every hour God gave. So I probably haven't been tough enough in going out and winning business.

Tony Player:
There's no question about that. Self-employment does bring an element of financial insecurity because you are totally dependent on not only the work that you are generating but ensuring it's profitable. You are not always in control of that; it's very often controlled by market forces.

But the longer you're in self-employment, if you've been moderately successful, then the more secure you become. And I think that in itself means you then become better, because whereas in your early days you make decisions based a lot on financial reasons later you're in a better position to make more sensible business decisions. You might leave one offer of a contract and be able to take a much better business decision to go for the better one, whereas in the early days you might grab the first offer that isn't so profitable and then not be able to take a later, better, offer.

But there is job security; the self-employed are more secure. You are master of your own destiny. You have got the ultimate decision about the way you run your life. But it's all also about risk. You normally find that somebody who is prepared to take the odd risk as a self-employed person is somebody that is likely to ultimately, if he knows what he is doing, take the right kind of risk.

When you first start up, assuming that you are of fairly tender years, you are going to go into it in a big way, the majority of people want to become big companies, million-aires and so on. That's certainly the way I embarked on it initially. But as you get older and more business-wise and more worldly-wise you begin to realize that you are possibly not going to become a millionaire, and there are things other than business that you should be thinking about; quality of life comes into the equation. And that enables you to make better business decisions. You are not just making business decisions because you want to become big and rich, you are making business decisions because it's the right thing for the company or the individual at the time. When I first started out, if somebody waved a job in front of me I'd find every reason to take it on. If somebody gave me an opportunity, I'd go for it. Now if somebody gives me an opportunity, somebody I don't know, the first thing I'll ask is: 'Why are they coming to me with a new opportunity?' And I do some background research. Are they coming to us because everyone else turned them down, and if so, why?

But you might earn £50 one week, you might earn £500 the next week. It's a difficult thing to control your life with that sort of variation of income. Maybe you've got a family to support. The average person in a secure job gets a regular wage every month and can plan his incomings and outgoings every month; he hasn't got the same sort of problem.

Reasons for becoming self-employed

Martin Attridge was driven into self-employment by redundancy. We asked how this might have affected his viewpoint.

I had a whole reaction to that particular circumstance; a kind of anti-organization reaction. I vowed never to join another organization. I think I've changed my mind on that somewhat because of the perennial insecurity of not knowing where the next piece of work is coming from. I guess my work tends to be only scheduled on about a 6 to 8 week basis. So I'm only looking at best a couple of months ahead. And that leads me, particularly when recessions are looming, to looking at joining an organization again. But that also brings its concerns. Any organization that I joined, if their business went sour, could get rid of me at a moment's notice at very little cost to themselves, and possibly at more cost to me in that I would have severed some links with my own clients and contacts.

I hadn't given a great deal of thought to becoming self-employed. I knew a number of people who had left employment and gone into self-employment with varying degrees of success. So really the redundancy was a spur to self-employment.

I think the picture painted of consultancy on the other hand is one of being able to do what you want with the people that you choose, and being able to take longer holidays, and so on. I guess it's undoubtedly true for some people but in my experience, and talking to a number of other individuals, it's not really the case. I think unless you've got a lot of stable work which enables you to see projected business for some time ahead then the reality is that most of us really live from hand to mouth to a certain extent. It's very difficult to turn down work of any nature.

The bad side of that is that you are forced to do things that perhaps you don't feel you have the skills or experience to do successfully. On the other hand I think it's remarkable what you can do when you are put in a tight corner. And that's what I've found. I have taken on a number of consultancy assignments that I wouldn't have done through choice a few years ago despite pretty much the same skill set.

Others have different reasons for moving out of employment into self-employment. We spoke to Sarah Francis, who set up her own telephone promotions company, about her decision to leave a lucrative job for the risks of running a business from home.

I was disappointed with the working world. And my decision to quit employment can be put down to a person that I worked with once. I got fed up with the unfair politics and backstabbing that went on in the company I was working for. I was dismayed that, irrespective of whether you do a good job or not, working environments could often be about the personalities involved, their egos, ambitions, and their abilities to influence others. It wasn't about the job or the work.

To me, work should be a place of fairness, where you enjoy spending your day, backed up with a good system of management and decent business practice. Perhaps that's too idealistic.

I discovered that role grooming, good support and management development isn't integral with every job. You're lucky if you get the right kind of nurturing. You know, a good mentor.

I was put off by selfish, self-centred individuals who couldn't give a monkeys about helping you grow and develop. And you couldn't choose the people you had to work with.

I had to work with one such individual and found it very hard to avoid being deeply upset and affected by the manipulative, untrustworthy, and deceitful behaviour I encountered.

I hadn't realized – until I left the company – how mentally exhausting it was to have someone trying to put you down at work all the time, criticizing your ability, your work output, your character, your personal life. This person's behaviour amounted to a concealed form of bullying, the likes of which I'd never experienced before. A condescending attitude towards me at every turn, punctuated only by the occasional attempt to befriend me (to gain information to turn against me).

Jealousy of my personal life and my progress at work, inventing lies, twisting truths to make themselves look good and me look bad were all part of the onslaught. It was an evil concoction. Even though I had the support of colleagues and friends at work, nobody could help me. Who needs a life like that?

After putting up with about four years of this appalling treatment, I took up a grievance with the senior management. They were supportive and sympathetic for a while, and 'knew what he was like'. They even made noises about making changes. But when it came to the crunch, they chose to ignore the negative sides of this person in favour of his work, which was generally good. So I was left to suffer it out.

Once I lost the support of the senior management, it was time to get out. Though I loved the work, I left and went self-employed. I don't want to work with people like that. I prefer to have more control of my working life, not to be suffering under someone like this character, nor to suffer the experience doubly when senior management turns a blind eye.

I can't say that going self-employed was a lifelong ambition. My bad experience in the employed world is actually what gave me the motivation to go for it myself. It was a bad thing which turned good.

James Wildman:
I liked having the security of having a job at 18 but I was made redundant at 22, and again at 23. I was, and still am, smarter than both of the managers that made those decisions and won't let it happen again.

My opinion now counts, something which as an employee it never did.

Tony Player took over the family business. His perspective is therefore a product of that:

There probably was an expectation that I should go into the family business. But initially I tried to avoid the family business because I didn't think it was what I wanted to do. I was in my late twenties before I joined it. But I had the opportunity to influence the nature of the business, so when I did go in it had become more akin to what I wanted to do. And then when I got in I changed it substantially in terms of the nature of work that it did.

But there was never direct family pressure; it was just lurking in the background. I could always have said no. In the end it got thrust on me by circumstance more than anything because I was in employment and it wasn't going too well, so I left. I knew that I could go and work for the family business as a stopgap and initially that's what I did. And it just went from there. But I had resisted the opportunity for ten years. Having said that, I think the pressure may well have got greater because my father ran the family business and he wouldn't let anybody take over from him. If I hadn't gone into it when I did the pressure would probably have become somewhat greater.

When I first joined it my father and I had different outlooks on the business. He is extremely, extremely reserved in everything that he does, that included his business life. I am not as reserved and I wanted to do something with the business as opposed to leave it where it was. We used to clash a lot. Not for the first year to eighteen months because I was a new boy and I just played a low profile. But then after I was more established in it we used to clash a lot, a hell of a lot, over the way that I saw the business going and the way that he saw it going. I think that clashing went on for about eighteen months to two years and in the end he decided, 'Well look, I'm getting to a point now where I've really got to take one step back and leave him to it.' So he took semi-retirement and just came in three days a week. And at that stage I took a more leading role and took over most of the decision-making. A couple of years after that he retired totally.

Other people's attitudes

We asked if those who were self-employed found that others were jealous of them, or pitied them the problems of running their own business.

Martin Attridge:
I don't think it's made a huge amount of difference really. But I guess my friends are now not the people that I once would have socialized with. I guess I now have more acquaintances than friends to be honest; the friends that I have are largely those that I knew in my schooldays.

But the world of work has changed so dramatically that people don't talk about being employed or self-employed. As one of my friends put it: 'I'm permanently employed when I've got a job, when I'm put out of a job I'm automatically self-employed and I go looking for work.' I think that seems to be true for quite a few people. I think several people I know have become rather more cynical about the whole work situation and what that means for individuals. There are no more jobs for life.

Onay Faiz:
My friends are envious of me, in the kindest possible way. My example has made all of them think about or plan to go

self-employed. They all tell me they're sick of the 'rat race' and the pressure to achieve targets all the time. Of course, you still have targets in self-employment. The difference is that you're in charge.

I'd even say that some of my closest friends are proud of me for taking the plunge. I don't think I've ever encountered pity from them except when I've been reported buried under 20,000 envelopes in my lounge somewhere.

Tony Player:
A lot of the people that I socialize with are self-employed business people, partners in companies, and they are in a similar situation to me. A lot of my old friends I don't see so much, I suppose they envy me to a certain extent, not because I'm self-employed, but because I earn a lot more money than they do. Take one person I knew from school, he works for [a major international company]. He's got standard earnings. Over the years I have met him once every couple of years or so and every time I meet him my personal circumstances have jumped on a bit. Even if you look at the sort of car I drive. Yes, I guess there is an element of envy there. But I took the chances, he didn't. He is still in the same employed position he was when he left school. That's the difference, isn't it? The difference between a self-employed and an employed person. Somebody that's a go-getter prepared to take risks and to take what it throws at you. I could never go and work for somebody; I would be totally unemployable.

Feelings of guilt

We asked if self-employed people felt guilty when not working.

Onay Faiz:
No. I figure my time is spent reasonably wisely and tasks are achieved as I want (most of the time) so I've no need to feel guilty when I take a bit of time off.

James Wildman:
Only someone who understands self-employment would

ask that question, and the answer is a big YES. I have to find a way not to.

Martin Attridge:
Not at all though I sometimes feel at a loose end. I think I normally work pretty hard when I am working. For example, I have just done four continuous weeks of training, three in Holland, one in the UK. Of those four weeks three weeks involved working with people I've never worked with before. So it's fairly taxing and I think because I earn reasonable money when I'm working then I feel I'm entitled to have time off when I'm not working. And also I think it's very necessary from a personal point of view. I need the space, I need not to do very much, I need to gather my thoughts.

What I think is quite difficult though is the change from the nine-to-five job which is pretty much at the same level month in and month out, compared to what I do which is a dramatic shift from not doing anything one minute, or doing different things, to suddenly having to get into work-mode at a high level. One of the skills of being self-employed is to be able to go in and out of those modes more quickly than you would as an employee.

Stress

We asked if self-employment had left people feeling more or less tired, and more or less stressed.

Martin Attridge:
Let me answer the second one first. Probably less stressed. Or at least, stressed for less of the time but then when I am stressed, stressed more intensively.

I think the most stress that I encounter is when I find pieces of work that I've been booked for have been cancelled and I may not get any money which causes a very negative reaction from me because it's money not going in the bank. And then I've got to try and work actively to try and replace that.

But I guess less stress because what is removed is the day-to-day frustration of working within a bureaucratic, non-productive, backward-looking unadventurous organization and you tell me one that's not like that . . . Tiredness. I'm very, very tired at times, but then I'm getting older as well! I find the travelling tiring, I find being away from home both stressful and tiring.

James Wildman:
It really is a different kind of stress, a better kind as you can change things and are basically in control. The worst kind of stress is when you have a problem and can do nothing about it – how I felt as an employee.

Onay Faiz:
I'm pretty stress-free, which is fantastic. That's not to say I never have a stressed day: I do. I'm a great believer in a little bit of stress is good for you, but the bad stress is gone. Because I'm in control of my working life and I can select the jobs and people I work with, stress has been controlled.

There is an awesomeness in taking sole financial responsibility for everything in my life. Knowing that your livelihood depends entirely on whatever you do in that office means you cannot afford to play about or let things drift. You have to make it work. That can be a good motivation. It can also be a hard pressure when you have your bad days. In employed work, if you have a bad week, you still get paid. Not so in self-employment.

My biggest difference has been learning to bounce back and carry on. Not giving up. Sometimes, when the brown stuff hits the electric spinning thing, and business has become very poor, with no money coming in, and bills awaiting payment, I've felt very down. I even wonder 'Is this wise to continue, maybe I should get a job.' But within a short time I've bounced back. I seem to be able to channel my energies into finding the next step and a solution.

As to tiredness, I would say 'less tired' simply as I get to choose my work hours and I pack them carefully with my jobs for each day. Because I'm not interrupted by phones and people in a huge work environment, I get lots of concentrated time for task completion. Also I haven't anyone else imposing unrealistic workloads on me. That means

I finish on time and get home on time. I'm less tired, and more satisfied with my day's work.

Tony Player:
It's more tiring because your mind is active all the time. Even if you are not actually at work your mind is active and that is inherently tiring.

As for stress: more stressed, but I think it depends on the circumstances at the time. If you're having a reasonable time at work and things are going well you're a lot less stressed because you haven't got anybody breathing down your neck. You make your own decisions. If things are getting tough and work is tight, margins are tight, and you're struggling to make ends meet then you get more stressed. I think the balance is probably fairly similar to if you are employed but the extremes are a lot greater; the highs are higher and the lows lower. I love the fact that you haven't got somebody breathing down your neck. I've got nobody to answer to; and that does release a lot of stress. But when things aren't going particularly well, you've got the weight of the world on your shoulders. You are the only one that's going to sort it out. You haven't got somebody else you can sort of step back and leave it to.

Mike Maynard and *Andrew Leigh*:
Mike: I think what I miss is what I had as a freelancer, as an actor. In those days when there was nothing on at all, my mind was clear, I could just relax. Nowadays I may have a day off but I've got the company in my mind, responsibilities and concern or anxieties about running the company that I never had as an actor. I may have had some fear about 'where is the next job coming from?' but basically my mind was clear. That doesn't happen any more.

Andrew: Research on stress suggests people get stressed because they don't have choices. Things are imposed on them. Freedom of action is impaired. I think that if the stresses of running the business can be identified they are all around feeling constrained and yet responsible. You are accountable but you actually don't feel you can do anything. For whatever reason you set up something but you are no longer able to control it in quite the same way.

Mike: But those responsibilities don't come from self-employment, they come from the role of being the boss. I know that for me my forthcoming absence through July and August is much about just being removed from the business long enough so that I can wake up in the morning and not have those things in my mind. That's actually my goal. When I go away for two weeks I know there's a point round about the second week where I don't wake up in the morning thinking MLA. And I just think it's unhealthy to wake up every single morning thinking MLA. So my two months away are about replacing thinking MLA with thinking, 'What am I going to create today in my life?'

Effects on home life

We asked how the structure of an office-based home affected home life.

Martin Attridge:
What is laughingly called an office is in fact half the kids' playroom and I defy you to identify where one starts and the other one begins. I think what you prompted me to think about probably is the pattern of work that I adopt when I'm at home. And to be quite honest I regard the working week potentially to be seven days in length. I certainly don't work a nine-to-five day. I work when I feel like it. And that often means I will do work sometimes on a Sunday afternoon if I choose to and then Monday afternoon I might go for a long walk. So I'm not terribly disciplined in that. I guess as with most people I work hard when I'm getting close to the deadline.

As for the children interrupting me: I think they know by my response when they can or can't interrupt me. They will interrupt, of course. But they're pretty good at respecting personal time. The other side of that coin of course is that if they need help and support then I need to make time to do that. So I guess it's certainly not me just saying, 'Look, I'm not going to be around for the next four days because I'm going to be working hard.' It would be very difficult for me to block out a whole evening if I wanted to produce a report when my children or my wife wanted to talk about something. It's about negotiating time slots for doing different things.

Onay Faiz:

My partner had to show a great amount of tolerance in having paper and envelopes and brochures everywhere, and in my taking over of his 'playroom'. Our house is only a small two-bedroomed place, so there isn't much luxury in space-availability. I had to do things like promise to clear the desk and floors of any files, books or papers every day, for when he came home. I found this a hard system to maintain daily, but it was a good discipline in organization for me.

I also started using his computer, which really put his nose out of joint, so we had to talk it over and negotiate computer slots for each other. I would have it all day, and he would have it all evening. We didn't have the space for two PCs in the house, so sharing was a necessity. He was very generous in sharing the computer with me, when he would have preferred not to. I would get a bit shirty when he, being in the computer software trade, would regularly change the entire system (I had no choice in this because it was his machine, after all) and tell me, 'It's easy'. What he didn't appreciate is that the constant changes of system slowed down my work immensely because I had to relearn the systems again. Being in the business, his aptitude was much faster than mine. If I didn't get it after a first showing, he made me feel rather dumb. How did we get over this one? I persuaded him to leave my software on the system as well as his adding new ones, and we increased the memory on the machine.

Satisfaction

We asked what was the most satisfying thing about being self-employed.

Martin Attridge:

Being totally responsible for a reasonably significant piece of work and seeing that to conclusion.

Onay Faiz:

It's a good few things for me. The ability to control my own work-time and workload, and, yes, be my own boss.

Getting good feedback from satisfied clients. I've always been very proud of the quality of my product. I'm fussy about giving a high-quality service. I know I could reduce my expenses by opting for cheaper suppliers, but that would mean giving the client a lesser quality product, and that I wouldn't like to do.

Sending out big invoices.

Taking those lifetime trips I've always dreamed about but never had enough holiday time to do it. I do it.

James Wildman:

Satisfying to have been self-employed for this amount of time – nearly ten years. And still being here that long after my business partner I set up with left after one year saying that it wouldn't work.

Sending out invoices – it's more satisfying than getting a pay cheque.

Tony Player:

I suppose the most satisfying thing that I have found is building a reasonable business. That if I hadn't been there it wouldn't have existed. Even when I went into the family business it was very small. I've made it bigger. It's successful now and because of my efforts. I get the most satisfaction out of that.

Having set the company up the way I have I can now easily spend a week, two weeks on holiday and it won't miss me. I've got the right people and the right controls in place. I get an element of satisfaction out of that.

Mike Maynard and *Andrew Leigh*:

Mike: I think this is the success. I think MLA has been a success. For us and those we work with and for. We've just celebrated our ten year anniversary.

Frustrations

We asked what was the most frustrating thing about being self-employed.

Martin Attridge:
The most frustrating thing to me, and this is maybe egotistical, is that I think I'm better than I project myself to be. And a lot of that is down to me; I should have had more work off my own bat, because I think virtually every assignment that I've undertaken people have been happy with.

Onay Faiz:
People who promise to pay up then don't, though I've never lost an invoice to the Never Paid Up Write Off file yet, which is good. The frustrating thing is that, particularly for small businesses, it only takes one large invoice to be paid late to really upset the cashflow. This has a bad knock-on effect including not being able to pay people you owe money to, which is a bit embarrassing. Big businesses don't care. They'll even employ people who specialize in delay tactics on payment of invoices! And there's little practical help us small business people can enforce to remedy the situation. I understand why small businesses fail on cashflow misfortune. It can be entirely out of your hands.

James Wildman:
Being told by financial institutions that you are unstable and worthless against someone was has a job and so-called security.

Tony Player:
Frankly, the most frustrating thing at times is dealing with people. When you're dealing with clients you expect to get frustrated; it's part of life. Everybody is looking after their own interests and you expect to have a certain amount of frustration dealing with suppliers and clients. But what I find the most frustrating thing is dealing with people that you've employed to do the job who are either not capable of doing it, not willing to do it or they are making your life as difficult as possible. I'm more than happy to pay the

going rate for the job; in fact we pay a lot more than our competitors. But having paid the going rate I want the job done properly and it's very difficult and very frustrating when you just can't get it done properly because people are not prepared to do what you expect of them.

Health

We asked if people had been more or less ill after they became self-employed. Had they had to cancel, or lost, work due to illness during their period of self-employment? How did this compare to when they were employed?

Martin Attridge:
Actually, going back to the time I was in employment I started to get quite ill then; stress-related I think.

But I find that since being self-employed I get ill when I'm working. For example when I'm working in Holland I often have a stomach complaint. I eat very little. I'm fine when I'm in the room with the students but I never feel content and settled outside that room, so I don't sleep well. I get stomach ailments and complaints. I lose weight. When I'm back I think it's like a recuperation period to me; it's almost like going away on holiday. It's not to say the cares of the world have disappeared but they are replaced by home-related issues which I feel are probably more manageable. I find it harder work as I get older, I think, to be honest. It is quite a lot of mental effort keeping on top of it.

Onay Faiz:
I was very rarely off with illnesses when I was employed. I'm very rarely off with illnesses now I'm self-employed.

The closest I've come to missing an appointment while self-employed was when I was a secondary attendee at a day's work (kind of a back-up, support person) but decided to leave after half a day because I was suffering heavily with a bad cold. I only chose to do so because I knew I could leave my colleague to continue in the primary role and because my absence wouldn't cause a problem.

James Wildman:
I've always felt very guilty taking time off work, this comes from working for my father for several years. If I do feel ill I might start late or finish early but almost never take a day off.

I've missed an appointment, but never a piece of work.

Tony Player:
I've got to be almost comatose before I won't go into work. I don't think about illness any more; illness just doesn't exist. If I wake up with a bloody cold or flu I still drag myself out of bed and go into work. And even if I don't go into work I'm still committed to it; I might be on the telephone or doing things at home. I don't think I'm now more or less ill than I was as an employee, but I am not prepared to have time off now. That's the difference really.

Regrets?

James Wildman:
My only regret is not having work colleagues – it's the hardest part.

Onay Faiz:
No, I don't regret going self-employed. It can be hard, when the cashflow goes belly-up and you don't know how you're going to pay the mortgage next month. It certainly has its hairy moments, but I love being in control of my own destiny.

True, I'm not a millionaire (yet), nor have I earned the same as peers who have got to higher levels at work and are earning good salaries now, but it's not all about earning lots of money. It's the lifestyle, too. And the lifestyle makes me very happy.

The only thing I miss a bit is more people contact. A lot of my work is solitary. I've always enjoyed the social aspects of working with people, not just for the chats over coffee breaks about home and work, the satisfying feeling of a good business meeting even, but also the feeling that you're part of something big and important. Working on your own, you can sometimes end up not seeing a soul for a day or two and feel like you're the only person on the planet! And your business sometimes seems awfully, awfully small.

However, I came up with the perfect solution. I set up a partnership business in addition to my existing one, and moved my business from home into a friend's office premises. He was beginning to feel the same as me running a one-man business, stuck out on a limb. He said he was feeling a bit stale from lack of company and a sounding board. We talked it over and felt we'd become more productive, not only as a joint business, but also in our own businesses simply because we shared an office. It worked. We've found that working together has brought a zest back into our creativity and we enjoy each other's company, too.

Professional advice

We asked what other professional advisors the self-employed had found useful.

Martin Attridge:
I think it was very important to get accountancy support. That certainly helped me manage things and anticipate things and make provisions in a much better way than I would otherwise have done.

I was quite heavily dependent on word processing services for the first couple of years. It wasn't until a couple of years ago, when I purchased my PC and started doing all my own report writing and typing, that I was freed from that need.

Financial advice is very useful. It's difficult to know quite where to get that from in terms of independence of support. The person who has best given me a vast amount is in fact my father who has taken a keen interest in his own finances and investments and has helped me there.

I haven't needed much bank support. I had my redundancy package to finance my start-up. But they've been OK.

Onay Faiz:
My best advice and help has come by networking with friends and managers in other businesses, asking them questions on their approach to particular things. I learned

a huge amount from my current partner when I watched him plan his business forecasts and budgets, and was involved in helping him with his presentation.

My accountant has been good at making me focus on aspects that needed attention in the business – it was him that recommended my computer package for small business budgeting.

My bank has never become very involved in my business. They've been pretty supportive on giving me an overdraft when I needed it. But I found that their views of businesses are very generalized. They were trying to give me advice which didn't quite gel with the nature of my business, and I knew such ideas wouldn't work. That was only one bank, mind. Maybe others have different or better business services.

What I have found is that you have to negotiate and push for favourable rates and better banking terms – they don't always reveal the most beneficial methods of running your account unless you ask or happen upon them.

Fellow small business people have been useful contacts, and we've passed business on to each other. Some of the local government initiatives, training and business support programmes can be useful.

James Wildman:
I achieved a loan from The Prince's Trust when I first started and they were the most help.

Skills and qualities

We asked what skills and qualities the self-employed had found they needed.

Martin Attridge:
You've got to be fairly entrepreneurial in that you can't be reliant on others as you would be in a hierarchical organization.

You've got to go out and seek work. You can't wait for the telephone to ring because it never does.

You've got to be pretty resilient. Things won't go the way that you'd expect them to go.

People won't pay up on time; you've got to be prepared to accept that and push hard to get your money.

To a certain extent you are laying yourself on the line and every time you are accepted for an assignment or you are turned down they are saying, 'Yes, we want you' or 'No, we don't'. So you've got to be able to take those knocks. You've got to be determined enough to see it through.

I think one thing that's particularly important where a lot of people fall down is that you have to be well-equipped to handle yourself firmly in terms of interacting with people.

One of the things that came across to me is that I found I had to be a lot sharper in terms of written skills, because by and large although I didn't have to submit a proposal for every piece of work I was going for I couldn't always rely on my relationship with someone I knew in the organization to get me the work; sometimes that person may not be the decision-maker. So all the other people will see of you is what you have written. And if you don't convey a good enough image, particularly for the larger blue-chip organizations, then you have no reason to anticipate that you will get work from them.

I think you've got to make some delicate decisions about degrees of openness and honesty that one uses. It could lose you a piece of business if you are too up-front, but some customers will respect you telling them all the things that are wrong with their organization and the reasons why they need you to help them.

It goes without saying that you have to be an effective listener to customers. Most of us listen reasonably well a lot of the time, but other times don't.

Business partnerships

Business partnerships are not always easy relationships. They are a lot like marriages: easy to get into and sometimes hard to live with and even harder to get out of. They have their ups and downs, and often suffer pressures from between the partners and further pressures from the partners' domestic relationships. We asked interviewees in partnerships for their observations.

Tony Player:

One advantage of having a business partner is that you discuss a lot of your problems with your partner and then you don't have to take quite so much home with you. Very often I'll sit down for half an hour, three quarters of an hour, after work and we'll just chat about things generally which means that by the time you have done that you don't want to go home and start talking again. I'm not saying that I don't talk about work at home, I do, but I don't tend to need to go into detail.

I wouldn't say ours is a 100 per cent relationship and it does get more difficult as we both get older. The biggest advantage that we have together is that my partner is more than happy not to take a front-line position in the business. He is not a decision-maker. He is more than happy to let me make the decisions. So although we've got a 50/50 share we've probably more like got a 70/30 share in terms of who takes responsibility on the board. If he was of the same personality as me we would have a serious problem. Because he recognizes that he doesn't take 50 per cent of responsibility I get the lion's share of the profit and a slightly higher salary. But this year when we were discussing it I got the impression that he thought he should be getting an equal share. The pressure comes from his wife; she has a strong personality. And a lot of the things that he says come out of his wife's mouth.

But the way I see it at the end of the day is that I'm happy with what I earn out of the business at the moment and for the foreseeable future. I see no reason not to be happy with what I earn out of the business. I am more than happy to give my partner a reasonable share out of what the business makes. I'm not out to share out every penny on a strict basis. If and when it comes to a time where he feels he is worth 50 per cent of the business then he will have to take 50 per cent of the responsibility as far as I'm concerned. Now the problem I have with that is that at that stage the business would then to a certain extent become non-functional. Then we would have clashes.

Mike Maynard and *Andrew Leigh*:

Mike: I think we respect each others' talents more than we do our own sometimes. I think I see Andy's talents beyond what I think he sees sometimes, and I think sometimes he sees mine beyond what I think I see. So we will sometimes hold a view of the other person, but it's bigger than they actually hold of themselves. Andy, he knows so much, you know. There is so much experience he brings to the partnership, so much information and expertise.

We don't spend a lot of time socializing. It was something that happened quite early on, I don't think we made any decision about it but it sort of emerged. And I think we felt that we stood more of a chance because of it. For me it stemmed from a personal thing where my Dad's partnership, which was with one of his life-long friends, broke up and it affected our personal lives as a family. I think there's a bit of me that was worried about that entanglement and sort of wanted it to be a bit cool around socializing beyond the ordinary friendship. Having said that I enjoy Andy's company and I enjoy spending time with Andy as a friend irrespective of whether we are talking work or anything, I just like being with him.

Andrew: I think it's avoided overexposure. Familiarity breeds contempt really. Overexposure would probably make it harder to make the thing work.

Mike: It started with me meeting Andy on a course, and hearing that he wrote books on management. I had an idea for a book on management. Andy was dissatisfied with his job and was looking to put some ideas of his own into action. So we got together in a business framework in the first place.

Andrew: What Maynard Leigh offered was the chance to put my ideas together in a new package.

Mike: I think the other thing we probably need to acknowledge, although it's odd, is that we are both Jewish. We are not religious Jews but we both come from a Jewish background. What that means genetically I don't know but there's something about the way we work, in particular our determination that may be cultural. We both have inbuilt guilt about the other one of us working harder!

Andrew: If in doubt feel guilty! It doesn't matter how hard I work, I know sometimes I do excessive amounts of stupid work, I still feel maybe I'm not quite doing enough. So I never feel that it's Mike not pulling his weight; quite the reverse. I feel that I am not pulling my weight. My worst fantasies are that Mike goes home to his wife and says, 'I don't think Andy is pulling his weight.' I always do quite a lot to prevent that. But I'm sure the reverse is also true; Mike feels he's the one not pulling his weight. The Jewish thing.

Mike: We are quite good at picking up when we are missing something. Often we will come to each other and say, 'I've been thinking about this', and the other person will say, 'God, it's brilliant you thought about that. I've forgotten. I hadn't been aware of that.' That little tiny thing is actually quite crucial.

And we often talk about the benefits of partnership; like when we are facing a problem, isn't it great to be able to share it with a partner. I think we sometimes forget that it's also so valuable that there is somebody else with their attention, their antennae out, their antennae pick things up that I think if you were a sole person you might miss.

Mike: I think the skills we have are complementary skills. We have never divided work into 'this is yours, that's mine' but it naturally happens by virtue of the different skills that we bring to the tasks in hand. And although our influence overlaps we are quite sensitive to intruding on an area where the other person has invested a lot of time or energy. Having said that, if one of us gets bored or stuck on something we can go to the other one and say: 'I can no longer go on with this area. Can you pick it up?'

We talk to each other, always. I think if you asked an outsider what happens between us they probably see us having quite a lot of heated discussions but I would say we have never had a row. I think they are very healthy.

Part of our initial discussion very early on was about our working together. We came up with this idea that if we had something that we were unhappy about rather than let it fester and build up as a resentment that we had a rule between the two of us, that we would always go to the other person within two weeks. We called it the two week rule. You had to go to the other person in two weeks and raise it. Or you had to forget it and get off it. And it was an either/ or. So there was none of this a year later saying, you know,

'And the other thing that really annoyed me about you is this . . .' And we still stick to it.

Business failure

And as a last subject for our interviews we discussed the personal effects of failure. When Tony Player's previous company failed, how had that affected him?

I lost total control of my finances for about six months. When the company went into receivership I didn't have a wage for six months. I didn't have enough personal wealth to be able to warrant that sort of length of time without an income. And I struggled; we were hit quite substantially, like I couldn't pay the mortgage. I eventually overcame that by re-mortgaging but I couldn't actually start drawing a wage for about six months until the other company that we created got up on its feet and I could get enough money out of that to pay a wage. I sometimes wished I could have thrown in the towel and gone into full-time employment but I couldn't because I had personal guarantees to fulfil to the bank. If I had gone into full-time employment I would never have got them off my back.

The thing with bankruptcy, or potential bankruptcy, you've got to go through it once to know how to handle it. And I didn't know how to handle it. It was traumatic. Most of my life for six months was actually living hell to the point where I didn't want to go to work in the morning. I literally didn't want to answer the phone when it rang. The first phone call that I had every single morning when I got into work was from the bank manager. And I knew it was always bang on nine o'clock and it was always bad news and it was always some sort of pressure. And the problem with that is, it's going to set you up for the day. The first phone call you have is a disaster phone call and the entire day just from that point on is just a nightmare. And that went on for about six months along with phone calls and creditors and people threatening writs and God knows what else.

We had a few nasty moments. The Revenue weren't as heavy as I expected them to be. They did give us some grace. But the VAT man was very heavy. In fact the VAT man was eventually the guy that forced us to make the decision to go into receivership.

Personal life was directly affected too. Although we were ex-directory some people found out the number and I had a couple of nasty phone calls at home. A couple of people turned up on the doorstep. One day I was driving home from work and my wife phoned me in the car and said, 'There's a bloke outside the house.' And I said, 'Well, I'll drive past and see who it is.' I drove past and didn't recognize him. In the end I drove into the driveway and got out of the car. And as I got out of the car he got out of his car. He got out the other side of the car and he had his hand down behind the bonnet. And I first thought he had a gun. He shot round the front of the car, and emerged with a letter in his hand. It turned out he was a bailiff or something, issuing a demand.

The whole process was a complete and utter nightmare. Having come out the other side reasonably successfully I look back at it and I think, 'I didn't handle it at all well.' Because I didn't know what to do. And I've now seen it happen to tons of companies, and everybody deals with it in separate ways.

The one thing I did have was good advice. I had an accountant that was very, very good. And because of his advice it meant that we could sort of get it all together and then continue on. Without his advice I would have had a big problem. But he told me at the beginning I would need balls of steel, and he was right.

I didn't actually have my house in hock to the bank, I had always refused to do that. I just had a personal guarantee. I had spent my entire life frightened of the bank. And right until our dying day they were still insisting that we put the house up and I refused; that was the best thing I ever did. The absolute best thing I ever did. All they were doing all the time was putting up the personal guarantee which didn't really mean a hell of a lot. I think we were up to a quarter of a million pounds in the end, personal guarantee, and there was no way they were going to get it. In fact in the end we just settled it for about £50,000. I think because they knew it was all they could get out of me.

I had no intention of ever paying it back to them; it came to a settlement. If we had had the house on the line I would have been under a lot more pressure.

So for six months I was really just doing nothing other than work. I mean, I couldn't play golf, my hobby, and if we went out socially all I was doing was thinking about work. Domestic life was just non-existent for me. I was going out of the house, getting in very early in the morning so at least I could do something before the phone started. I wasn't going home until eight, nine o'clock at night. I was going in Saturday and Sunday. I wasn't sleeping, I couldn't sleep.

It took a hell of a lot out of me. A hell of a lot. For one thing I think it affected my memory. I can't remember anywhere near as much as I used to. Before that started I never used to have a diary; I used to remember everything, exactly what I was doing, where I was going, I never even bothered with a diary. I can't remember anything now. I have to have a diary and write everything down.

The stress was so great I used to get into bed and within about half an hour everything that I wore or had around me was saturated. Sheets were wet, clothes were saturated. Every night that was what I used to go through. In the end I did the typical thing; I just hit the bottle, I got on the Scotch. Then I could get about three hours sleep. But I came through it.

But having been through it, been through the experience, if – heaven forbid – I ever had to go through it again I would know exactly how to deal with it.

In the long run it was a very, very good business experience. You sort of put it away in the memory bank and very often you refer back to it and I think it helps you to make good decisions.

But I can tell you, the biggest relief of my life was the receivers arriving on the doorstep. I could tell the staff what I had been keeping from most of them, and the pressure was off.

The question of business failure, and personal bankruptcy, which Tony's description brings to mind allows us to make the point that while many people see bankruptcy as a demon, the great nightmare scenario to be avoided at all costs, it can be an opportunity for a fresh start. There are many successful business-men who have suffered a bankruptcy in their past. Approximately 20,000 people go bankrupt every year, 1993 held the record at 31,000.

So what is bankruptcy, and what are its implications?

A bankruptcy order is made, by the courts, when the court is satisfied that debts have no likelihood of being repaid. It is a myth that a bankrupt cannot then borrow money; though there are limitations. An undischarged bankrupt may not borrow more than £250 unless he has informed the would-be lender that he or she is bankrupt. If a lender who has been given that knowledge then chooses to go ahead with a larger loan, that is quite legal.

It is also a myth that bankrupts may not have bank accounts. In fact they are entitled to, though they may find banks uncoop-erative. And undischarged bankrupts may need the agreement of the Official Receiver to open a new account.

Another belief is that bankrupts may not run another business. That is also not correct. It is an offence to carry on business in a different name from the name in which they were made bank-rupt if they fail to notify all those with whom they do business that they have been bankrupt. However, bankrupts may not be directors of limited companies, nor run one directly or indirectly.

Bankruptcy generally lasts three years, after which they will be discharged, and released from their debts.

3 / SWOT Test Yourself

THOSE THINKING OF becoming self-employed should do the following SWOT analysis as a starting point to determining their own fitness for the rigours of running their own business.

SWOT stands for Strengths/Weaknesses/Opportunities/Threats. It examines those aspects of self-employment which the individual sees as being one of those characteristics. They are often counterparts; the opposite of a strength is a weakness for example. What one person regards as a threat another will regard as an opportunity. SWOT examines how you react to challenge. Overall, it gives pointers to how you will find success, and how you will avoid failure.

How do you rate?

The following are typical aspects that arise when the self-employed or the likely-to-be-self-employed do a SWOT analysis. Check yourself off against these lists. And do you own analysis – now, and continue to do it throughout self-employment.

Strengths

- *Professionalism.* A chance to demonstrate your professionalism to others, to capitalize on your skills to carve out a path of your own.
- *Focus.* The focused person has the best chance of succeeding. The days and weeks and years of self-employment are filled with highs and lows. Often it takes tunnel vision of where you want to be, and how you intend to get there, to keep on track.
- *Self-motivation.* Those who find they cannot start work in the morning unless someone else is driving them are going to find

self-employment an uphill struggle. Self-motivation includes confidence, a desire to win, and setting goals. If self-motivation is your strength a good many battles are already victories in the making.

- *Tenacity in the face of disappointment.* There will be plenty! Orders that don't materialize despite promises. Contracts that do not get signed up even after months of negotiations. Unfairness. Red tape. Refusals by banks and creditors to see the world the way you do. Promised cheques 'lost in the post'. If you cannot 'pick yourself up, brush yourself down and start all over again' regularly, if you cannot replace anger with the occasional wry smile, and if you take every obstacle personally, you would be wise to give up now before you dig yourself into an early grave.

- *Belief that you have something to offer.* The world beats a pathway to the door of the person with the new mousetrap. But it also beats pathways to those who package the old mousetraps differently, and who sell them to people who didn't know they needed a mousetrap. The only people the world ignores are those with no novelty. What is it that you've got that makes you different? A product? A service? A new way of delivering either? A new pricing structure? A new trading deal? If you don't have something special to offer then how do you think you will attract your customers away from those who supply them already? But don't be disheartened: there are always opportunities, you just have to find them. Start listing a few under 'Opportunities' right now. If you can't think of anything to put in that section in the next week throw this book away and go out and get an employed job!

- *Confidence.* As the saying goes: 'Whether you think you can, or whether you think you can't – you're probably right'. Before Roger Bannister broke through the four-minute mile there were those who believed it simply could not be done; after he did it the list of those who followed him grew quickly. Having seen it done others then acquired the confidence of knowing it *could* be done. And confidence is a factor of persistence, and of risk. Both of which you are going to need in abundance in the years ahead.

- *Marketing of self.* If there is a single area where the self-employed fall down it is in marketing. They have the right product or service, and they package it well. But they do not always find the buyers. The self-employed are constantly on display in their own 'shop window'; they need to market their own qualities to the world at large. Very few self-employed people grew their businesses while hiding behind the pot plants. They grew by having confidence in themselves and making sure everyone else knew it and heard about it. Self-employed people are sometimes thought of as 'pushy'; but some 'pushiness' is necessary.

- *The ability to finish work.* It is astonishing how many employed people have piles of work around their offices that are 99 per cent finished but just waiting for that last bit of paperwork to be completed. Or just waiting for that last meeting to finalize this or that aspect of the work. The ability to finish work is lacking in many people. But self-employment often needs that ability – the invoice can't go out until that last 't' is crossed and that last 'i' dotted, and the invoice is how you get to eat next week! You will need to be – or learn to be – a finisher.

- *Continual expansion of the product or service base.* It is a tenet of business that when you have found a unique product, or a unique service, or a new way of delivering either, then someone will be breathing hard down your neck. However good you are now someone is – right now – working out a way to be better. All that other person needs is for you to rest on your laurels and think you've won the war – and you just made yourself a loser. Never be complacent. Keep an eye on the rear-view mirror. And remember Churchill's adage: if you want peace, prepare for war.

- *Ability to work on your own.* Every self-employed person emotionally works alone. Some are in partnerships of course. Some have significant teams working for them and around them. But when you wake up in the middle of the night your business will not be far from your mind, and at such times you are alone. The self-employed think alone at times, they have to act on their own instincts, they have to know that the buck not only stops at their desk, but in fact never left it. If you want a 'mothering' company around you to protect you from the ravishes of the corporate world then get an employment and don't even think about self-employment.

Weaknesses

- *Perfectionism.* Perfectionists might well think of their trait as a strength rather than a weakness, but the self-employed soon discover the fallacy in that argument. The level of quality of a job should be set by the job, not by some abstract belief that can be applied to all tasks. For example, in a written report there is clearly a difference between a memo inviting a few office colleagues to a departmental night out and the text of the glossy brochure which will be used to promote the company to potential clients for the next two years: the odd punctuation mistake and less than perfect wording in the former does not matter as much as in the latter. But we know of those who pour hours of effort into getting even the former absolutely correct, even commented on by others before distribution. The self-employed soon find that this is an indulgence they cannot afford, that corners will need to be cut at times and that it is best to get into the habit of knowing where the corners are that can be safely, legally and unembarrassingly cut.

- *Overplanning.* The self-employed need business plans and forecasts if they are to succeed, but there comes a point where overplanning is the sign that the individual has lost the plot somewhat! Two examples from actual situations we have seen come to mind. The first was a small partnership of three people being set up in a consultancy field. They came to our accountancy practice with a proposal and forecast for their company set out in admirable detail; it ran to 97 pages. It gave detailed descriptions of potential clients and contracts and had a very detailed cashflow forecast over the next two years running alone to fifteen pages. We have no criticism of this as the reader will discover in a later chapter of this book on business plans. But the partnership issued updates in increasing detail (115 pages at the end – we kept them all as a case study!) each month for four months despite the fact that not one contract had been signed up. Enquiries revealed that the partners were spending an astonishing amount of time planning and forecasting running to days per week – when they should have been putting the maximum energy into getting work and income. Their problem was that they were doing what they knew how to do and avoiding what they needed to do – to sell themselves. We advised them to do so, and work came in within the next two months. And, predictably, once they had better things to do and they were properly up and running the management reports diminished down to around fifteen pages a month – good, concise 'need-to-know' stuff. They had found the right balance. The second case was of a former Account Manager for a multinational company who decided to try his hand at self-employment (but who frankly had few of the necessary qualities and who has since gone back to full-time employment where he is very well thought of and well remunerated). He spent a week researching his office furniture for his home, getting just the right desks and so on. He spent ages in libraries getting the best management books (not one of which he actually read). And he spent nearly £3,000 on courses to teach him how to be a high flyer in business, on how to lay out his office using feng shui to give him the best environment, and so on. But he spent not a minute on getting clients. Then he compounded the problem by employing a secretary (for whom he had no work) and an assistant (whose only work consisted of moving the office furniture around). Part of his problem was that he had a large cash reserve to indulge himself with – the 'breath of the poorhouse on your back' is the great motivator he was lacking. The other problem was that he needed the environment of his former office – the big mother ship surrounding him, and he needed support staff. In truth, we think he was also hiding from the inevitable day when he had to go and find clients. In his previous employment (and his current one) he was given the contacts already 'warm' and he developed them, which was his skill. He was, it seems, hopeless at getting them from cold which the self-employed must be able to do. The final clue came when he admitted that prior to employing an assistant he hadn't had a cup of coffee in his office (in his home, remember!) because during work hours he had no one to go out and get one and no-one to make one for him. He seemed taken aback at the suggestion that he could always go and make one himself – he really didn't seem to have thought of that. Of course planning is essential to success, and setting up the right environment before the work pours in is possibly the best chance you will get before 'all hell breaks loose'. But there must be a balance and many spend a disproportionate time *planning* and not *doing*.

- *Losing interest.* Are you the sort of person who cannot sustain an interest for more than a few months or years? Such people are often very suited for employment where promotion and change mean new outlooks and new horizons constantly on offer. But self-employment, while offering great variety, does not offer such great opportunity for change. 'Keeping at it' for years building and developing a business is essential. You have to be in for the long term, prepared to stay 'in the same job' in effect for many, many years if not in some ways for life. Think about self-employment, for this point anyway, as constraining you to a time of work for twenty years with no chance of jet-setting business trips or huge promotions and job-changes. Does it still feel good? If you enter self-employment thinking that in five years things will look very different you may be wrong (in some trades and professions anyway). Know what you're getting into, and whether it suits you.

- *Self destruction.* It is almost an extension of the point above, but are you self-destructive? We can illustrate this with the case of one interviewee, Martin, who has started at least a dozen businesses in the last few years. They are not unsuccessful, it's just that he destroys them himself. He starts a business, works long hours often neglecting his family in order to build it up, creates a space for himself in his chosen market, and then becomes attracted to some quite different line of business. To pursue this, he ignores the first and it eventually collapses or just 'tapers away'. And then he will do the same for a third, and a fourth, and so on. We suggested to him that it was the thrill of the chase rather than the marriage of himself to his business that he desired most. That seemed even more evident when he admitted that that was certainly his character trait with women – many short-term relationships usually ended when he went off with another woman, and currently he was living in his fourth marriage. He could not, however, accept that he was applying the same attitude to his business life and offered many reasons why his businesses failed or had been closed down by him. But whether we should criticize this or not we're not sure about; perhaps he has found the one way to be self-employed and meet his own inner needs. Perhaps he should be a further category in Chapter 1!

- *Getting side-tracked into areas where you are not skilled.* Wanderlust as described above can lead the self-employed individual into areas where they are not going to be as successful as they have been because they are getting out of their depth. Diversity, new concepts and so on are important, but they take careful planning and often the introduction of other people into the business to make it work. Consider diversity very carefully; treat it as a new business. If you didn't have the 'core' business to start from would you start up a business from cold in this new area, risking your money and time? If the answer is no, then ask again why you think you can make this gamble work now. If the fact that you have a reserve of cash behind you is the only reason, then you must re-plan. Do a new business plan. Having money behind you can be a disadvantage. As the old saying goes: 'The only certain way to walk out of a casino with a small fortune is to have walked in with a large one.'

- *Getting seduced by money rather than product/service.* If the goal of self-employment is only to make money then you probably will not succeed, though it is a sensible goal to have in the list. But you must be genuinely committed to your product or service, want to deliver it, want to meet your clients' needs. Otherwise someone else will come along and do what you do better. They might even charge more for it, and make more money, but it will be because they thought of the reason for the work rather than just the money at the end of the process.

- *Falling in love with the client so that you cannot be objective.* To illustrate this take the example of one consultant we interviewed who had a long-term contract with a major national company. His job was to do what those inside the company culture could not do – challenge the company and its people. His problem was that he was there so long he was really just another one of the staff in all but name. And he had lost so many other opportunities for work that he was now so afraid of losing that client that he couldn't do the very job he was engaged to do – which was to risk their wrath by challenge!

- *Not knowing when to walk away/change direction.* There comes a time when you have to move on, or redirect your thinking. If you cannot do this you will fall behind in what is needed in the marketplace and you will fail to take opportunities even if you see them. One interviewee, Ivan, had successfully built up and sold two businesses. The third business revolved around one product in the Human Resources Management field. The product was identified as being a potential winner and attracted substantial venture capital. But despite building a sales force and substantial interest being shown by major companies the product did not actually sell. The initial interest did not convert into income. At this point, as Ivan stated, he should have walked away but in fact he continued with product development, marketing and sales, until there were no funds left to pay the bills. The company went into liquidation.

- *Inability to delegate to people or machines – trying to hold too much in your head.* A business can only be as big as the brains that hold it. If everything is in your brain then that is the limit of your business. Delegate to others to free yourself so that you can take the business to the next stage. This can be delegating the thinking, or the doing. A decorator that will not allow anyone else to do work for him because he believes that he alone can maintain quality cannot grow his business. When you cannot delegate any more – and in truth there is *nothing* that you cannot delegate! – then you have reached your business limit. We examine delegation in more detail in Chapter 4.

- *Being over-cautious – not a risk-taker.* Business is about taking risks. You have to sell to people on credit and you risk not being paid; you have to try new products and services in the marketplace but some might not be successful; and so on. If you cannot take risks then you cannot play in this game.

- *Not setting stretched targets for self.* Some people coast. They are making enough money, they have a routine, and it is comfortable. Why push themselves? Perhaps that is fair and they should be left alone, but certainly there are many who do not reach their full potential because they decide to stop trying, to stop taking risks, and rest on their laurels. If you want to really find your full potential set hard targets and be ready to fall at a few. Failure is your proof that you're pushing yourself to your limits. Failure is a very positive indicator because of this.

- *Being too wrapped up in the product.* Clive Sinclair's commitment to his C5 electric car was probably essential to its ever being made at all, but a little less commitment in that case might have relieved him and the world of a dead-end. Nuff said!

- *Not recognizing the opposition is catching up*. Rose-tinted glasses are not useful in business. As the makers of the James Bond films recognized, however good you are the opposition will come along and do what you do better. You have to be very nimble to keep ahead of the field.

Opportunities

- *Ability to manage your own life*. Although self-employment does not put everything in your life in your absolute control it can go a long way. In some cases you can decide when to work, and build work around your family and friends. You can decide who to work with, how to work to suit yourself, and so on.
- *Ability to develop new skills*. Self-employment brings out the best in people most of the time. Challenge (or desperation, in some cases!) forces you to draw on talents you never would have otherwise released. And it forces you to get training in areas you would have ignored, all of which is exciting. It is also useful for your career path if you choose to go back to employment.
- *Working from home – or in some way that suits you*. If you have the kind of business that can be done from home here's the chance to commute no further than from the bedroom to the office downstairs. For some it is a dream, for others a nightmare. But the choice is always yours.
- *Choosing your hours*. The self-employed, they say, only have to work half a day – and you can pick your own 12 hours!
- *Ability to balance business and family*. Too many people, some would argue, miss out on the formative years of their childrens' development and by the time their career or business is successful enough for them to relax and take a step back the young ones have flown the nest. For many, self-employment is a way to be with your family and not miss out on one of life's 'special offers for a limited time only'.
- *Being answerable to yourself*. You have the chance to 'do it your way' and take the consequences without interference from others. Even failure can feel good if you know that you have 'had a go' that you would have regretted missing out on all your life. And from failure will come future success if you're persistent.
- *Choice of who you work with*. This can be a big one for some –

Not having to work with unpleasant people, perhaps not having to work for unpleasant clients and customers. For many, stress arises from having to work with people they don't get on with – you may be able to reduce or eliminate that stress at least.

- *Making a wide variety of contacts and friends.* Although we have said that the self-employed are emotionally alone, clients have told us that their relationships with people expand all the time and for many it is one of the pleasures to meet new, interesting people all the time instead of working each day in the same workplace with the same faces around you.
- *Ability to grasp any nettle; to take any chances.* You never have to miss a chance because someone else said 'no'. You won't always win, but you will always know that you took the gamble. And you'll love the ones that do win.

Threats

- *Letting business dominate and losing your social and family life.* We have seen a lot of successful businesspeople lose their spouses, families and friends in the pursuit of work and more work. Friends and relatives can become less important than a new client-contact. Can you get the balance right?
- *Wandering from your spouse!* That large network of contacts offers opportunities for infidelity. Perhaps more than most employments, the wide range of new contacts in self-employment seems to encourage a few with wanderlust – in this case with the emphasis on lust – to wander. We've seen a lot of self-employed people take up relationships with their clients. And usually in the end losing both the social and the business relationship.
- *Losing your nest egg.* If you go into self-employment because you have a lot of money, perhaps from redundancy or inheritance, then you have only one of many necessary factors. If you haven't thought through much more – as detailed in this book – then you might as well take the short cut and just throw the money into the nearest drain.
- *Remortgaging to keep the business going.* Often the self-employed have to put their own valuable assets at risk as part of the 'deal', perhaps signing their house over to the bank to secure a loan. If the business goes down, you might find yourself losing

your home. Are you ready for that risk? Have you discussed it as a family?

- *Losing regular income.* When the money rolls in self-employment feels like a pot of gold at the end of the rainbow. But what about when it does not? When a month goes by with no income, just a drain on personal savings? Are you ready for a financial roller-coaster ride. More white-knuckle than a theme-park some months!

- *Refusal to face reality.* When the business is going wrong people go off into Walter Mitty-land and refuse to acknowledge the problem. If you don't think you can be realistic and self-critical then you are lacking a vital quality of self-employment. An ostrich with its head in the sand never grew a business.

- *Inappropriate purchasing – too fast and flashy a car too early.* One mistake of some self-employed is to take 'the rewards' too early. In the case of some businesses, particularly in manufacturing or areas needing constant capital expenditure, most of the money generated in the first few years needs to be ploughed back. That middle-of-the-range car you're dying to get rid of will just have to be patched up for a few months yet. And when your wife asks 'What shall I do with my old clothes' tell her 'Keep wearing them!'

- *Forgetting to generate income because of enjoying the work too much.* Spending too much time on what is fun and not what makes the money come in. Despite an earlier warning that money is not the only focus – product and quality being essential others – if you don't make money you go bust. It is a good idea to make client contacts perhaps on the golf course, but if you think four days on the course and one in the office is a good balance you're probably in for a shock. Wait until you see the handicap your bank manager gives you!

- *Becoming disillusioned by now being unemployable.* Self-employment is a seductive mistress. You are pampered by the choices you have, and the lifestyle you can create. But the downside is that if you have to leave self-employment you may by now have become unemployable: unable to play the 'company' game, follow the rules, do as you are told, etc.

Every strength is a potential weakness, every opportunity is a potential threat; how you deal with circumstances is part of being the right kind of person for self-employment. Keep checking your SWOT periodically – it keeps you on your toes.

Good luck.

We asked one of our interviewees, Onay Faiz, what she had learned about herself during her self-employment; what strengths, what weaknesses, what responses to situations she had found in herself.

I can't say I discovered any sizzling new talents. I think I went into my business with a fair idea of my strengths and weaknesses. If anything, being self-employed made me recognize and work harder to improve my weaknesses. It also forced me to capitalize on my strengths.

I've an instinct for whether I could cope with a challenge even if I then have to work out how – I've taken some of my biggest business risks like that, some were successful, some not. I'd be lying if I said I never felt like running away from some challenges I've been forced to take: like phoning the bank to ask for an increase in my business loan. There have been occasions when during bad times (for example when a marketing campaign failed to bring the results I wanted and needed, or people haven't paid up on time and thrown my cashflow into chaos) I've felt like escaping from it all. But that's only when I can't see a solution. I've always managed to come back with a solution in the end. So far.

I'm much calmer and happier as a person. I'm very disciplined about my work and have a strict working day which I plan out very carefully to ensure I achieve productive tasks which will bring in money.

Despite working from home, come 9.00 a.m., my mind goes into work mode and I have no trouble maintaining a working sense for the whole day. I never allow myself to wander off and clean the loo, or finish last night's washing up. I was at work, and whilst there, home life was on hold until 5.30 p.m. While I've been self-employed, the division has always been very clear to me.

I've also found I can switch off very easily. The moment I close the door to my office at home, and take my journey home (down a flight of stairs to the lounge!) that is my work day over. I rarely bring problems 'home'. When I was employed, I came home with them all the time.

I've always shrunk away from this term in job ads, but I guess I must be a self-starter.

James Wildman told us:

I don't know if self-motivation is a talent but I found out that I have it. I found out that I can generally be very happy working on my own.

Richard Grossman is a well known stockbroker and Freeman of The City of London. He is a success story and he readily admits that he had no great plan to get where he is now.

Richard left school at 16 after O Levels and studied to be an accountant before joining the family textile business in Yorkshire. After a couple of years of being 'the boss's son' he decided to go it alone and like Dick Whittington came down to London to join the City. Starting as a clerk in the back office settling stock transfers, Richard progressed through the traditional route of junior clerk to becoming a dealer and member of the Stock Exchange. At this time Richard became one of the youngest councillors of Westminster City Council. Driven by an enjoyment of City life as well as life in general, and the desire to do the best by his family, Richard moved through various broking houses, survived Big Bang and is presently an independently self-employed stockbroker as well as heading up the London office of Redmayne Bentley, a well-respected broking house with offices throughout the UK.

Talking through Richard's modesty it was evident that his success was due to a number of factors, many unrelated but as a mix a good indicator of the drives and skills needed to survive and win in the financial jungle. They are as follows:

- An overriding love of the stockbroking business, with the challenges of the market and the ability to interact with clients.
- The drive to be self-employed, with the freedom it can afford.
- The basic core values of honesty, integrity and humour.
- A flair for recognizing talent, then recruiting and retaining those who have it.

- The vision to look for the next opportunity to develop himself and the business.
- An impatience with fools but not rudeness.
- The need to want to get out of bed to go to work even after a late night.

4 / Core Skills of Self-Employment

Time management

Workwise, a major difference between being self-employed and an employee is that employees are often time managed by their organizations whereas self-employed people have to manage their own time. (Though, interestingly, empowered staff in modern companies are in more control of their own time than is often realized. They are given an agreed budget and objectives and how they spend their day, week, month is up to them, so long as they deliver their objectives on time, within budget and at the agreed measurement of results.) However, the self-employed have no-one to fall back on for advice when time management goes awry.

Time management is a personal attitude about how you are going to spend a very scarce and inelastic commodity. The secret of time management is to develop a personal sense of time, its value, and how you are going to apply your time to the objectives and results you have set yourself. Therefore the first stage of managing time effectively is to set realistic goals and targets and monitor them against your time frame and keep an ongoing record of how you are actually spending your time.

Self-employed people are by nature highly motivated – at least they need to be! – and this can lead to becoming a workaholic, causing problems for the individual, the family, relationships and friends. One of the rewards of being self-employed is the ability to be in control of your own life, so right at the outset a balance must be drawn between work and your life outside work.

Beware, also, the 'activity trap', where you apply all your energies into the things you *like* doing such as developing marketing literature on your desktop computer. Don't put off the things you *hate* doing such as debt collection. It all needs to be done. It is very easy to convince yourself that you have had a busy day – but have you had a productive day?

The three primary stages in managing your time are:

- Periodically review how you are using your time by recording it in a simple time diary. You can make these up yourself or purchase a time recording system from good stationers. Record your time for a week, three to four times a year.
- Then critically diagnose the use of your time, by determining why you are doing a particular task, what would happen if it were not done, and if what you are doing significantly contributes to your goals and objectives.
- Organize the use of your time, delegate what can be delegated, cut out or at least reduce time-wasting activities and concentrate time on the productive tasks.

Time management is about being selfish and in control. Kirsten Klingels is an accomplished freelance violinist who has recently toured China, Turkey, Germany and other European countries as well as fulfilling a very busy diary in the UK. Managing her life includes consideration for her husband and daughter, keeping house, practising her music, attending auditions and learning new scores. When asked how she manages, her philosophy is encouragingly simple:

> Concentrate on what needs to be done, be selfish, with a smile, meet your goals, even if the housework does not get done, and rediscover take-away meals.

Always allow time for what you are doing, give yourself thinking time, do not hurry and do not try to do several things at once. Remember that stress at work is usually not caused by what you have done, but more often by what you have left undone.

Negotiating skills

Negotiating is about trading, and basically the trade-off equation is: I get something I want. In return you get something you want.

In day-to-day business trading is conducted through money,

although sometimes under a barter system such as products for products, services for services. Self-employment means that you have to negotiate for products and services as well as selling your products and services. In our commercial society it is relatively easy to establish a price for goods, services or time, as these are determined by the market place. However, daily we have to negotiate with people, whose negotiating skills are unknown and new to us.

We all have a degree of negotiating skills which we learn from the moment we are born, and continue to learn and refine all through our lives. People who are good negotiators have discovered that they really enjoy the game and are often highly trained in the process. Starting-points for a negotiating position are recognizing the value of your product or service in the market place and having a sense of what your time is worth. This is difficult: footballers earning £20,000 a week will have an agent or manager to negotiate for them, whereas a qualified teacher on £20,000 a year cannot directly negotiate in the public sector. It is also useful to remember that we do not always enjoy negotiating, and many people will be uncomfortable negotiating an increase in an overdraft, selling a house or car, or negotiating for unemployment benefits. However, self-employment means that you have a duty to yourself to maximize the value of your time and effort as much as giving a quality service or product.

In any negotiating position we must recall that both sides have degrees of influence and power, and levers they can use to get what is called their most favoured position. When purchasing a motor car the salesperson wants to sell you a car. The original starting price is only the entry point, the negotiation is about you gaining something, i.e. a price reduction, or a sun roof, etc., and the salesperson trying to retain as much commission as possible as well as meeting a bonus target. Trying to establish the other person's most favoured position takes time and research to uncover the other party's weaknesses and strengths, both a good investment. Common sense also comes into play: for example, the best time to negotiate a price for central heating is in the middle of a hot summer's day.

Let us now consider some ideas on how to negotiate:

- Prior to the negotiating meeting set yourself and apply minimum and maximum limits, i.e. the bottom line on what you are prepared to sell at, or buy at.

- Work out your signals in advance, e.g. how you are going to dress, your degree of openness, language style, or eye contact. When visiting your bank manager, clean neat working clothes give a better impression of who you really are at work than the left-over wedding suit.
- Allow plenty of time for the negotiations. Shortage of time often leads to a 'no'.
- Remember always to seek a win-win outcome.
- Stick to the issues in hand and do not lead or be led into personal disclosures about your circumstances which can have an effect on the outcome. For instance, do not tell the other party that you have no work at the present as this will encourage the other party to knock you down on price.
- Do not lose your temper or show irritation, or defend your motives as described by the other party.
- Speak clearly, slowly and quietly. Give way to the other party's interruptions. Do not give or react to veiled threats or other pressure.
- Understand who you are negotiating with, their personality, culture, values, ego, etc.
- Try and establish friendship, very useful of course for long-term trading relationships.
- Use the broken record technique, i.e. keep repeating your win-win argument, e.g. I do wish to sell you my products, however, you must help me on the price.

Negotiating, like any other skill, can be learned from experience, practice and training. Learn from your mistakes. If you don't get the sale, contract or work, ask why? Develop your skills and above all learn to enjoy the game.

Powerful presenting

In our experience as trainers in this field, most people do not like giving presentations. This does not however preclude them from doing a good job. As self-employed people you will often have to give presentations to buyers, panels, committees, customers and clients in order to sell your products and services. Powerful presenting is an exercise in persuasion, together with planned preparation, effective speaking and eye-catching aids such as brochures, samples and computer-generated visuals.

Like any good story your presentation must have a hard hitting beginning, an informative and interesting middle, and an enthusiastic and selling ending. The ending is most important as it is the last thing your audience will remember. Never forget the old adage that any fool can start a love affair, but it takes a clever person to end one. The basic aim of presenting is to get the other people thinking like you, by positively selling the benefits of what you are offering, demonstrating your knowledge of the product and service, and matching them to your customer needs. The following guidelines we have found invaluable in training and coaching in presentations:

- Start confidently and with enthusiasm.
- Relax and adopt an easy and friendly manner.
- Do not speak for too long without a break. Ten to fifteen minutes with questions is about right and will fit in with the concentration span of the average person.
- Always make the presentation relevant to your audience by telling them something they do not already know. We are all guilty of sometimes telling people what they already know.
- Learn to control the signs of your nervousness and avoid mannerisms that will annoy or irritate the audience, e.g. jangling coins in your pocket.
- Speak to all the audience, establish good eye contact, do not stare anybody out, and do not stare into space or at the floor.
- Always give way to questions, and answer honestly. If you don't know the answer to a question say so, offer to find out, and ask if anyone in the audience can help. Remember the person asking the question probably knows the answer, otherwise they could not have formed the question, so ask the questioner for their views and build on them. It builds relationships.
- Avoid jokes unless you are really good at them, but try and inject humour into your talk where you can.
- Do not tread on other people's values, attitudes or beliefs.
- Use 'the pause' to emphasize your main points.
- Use expression in your voice to make it sound more interesting.
- Avoid jargon, technical terms, or other specialist language that could confuse or lose the attention or comprehension of your

audience. (Unless you are certain of the make-up of that audi-ence where your knowledge of their 'inner' language may help form a bridge between you.)

- Use the buddy system, i.e. take with you to your presentation a colleague, partner or friend to support you. Give your buddy six questions to ask you first in case you dry up. Your buddy can also give you signals as you go along, e.g. speed up, move along, slow down, etc. These can be executed by hand signals agreed before the presentation.
- Always dress your best, it will give you confidence.
- Never be late – and start on time.
- If you don't know what you are talking about, don't talk. Therefore there is no substitute for preparation. We recom-mend strongly that all presenters prepare a talk plan, and the one we favour is often referred to as the 'John Wayne method' of communication:

Tell 'em what you're going to tell 'em.
Tell 'em in detail.
Tell 'em what you've told 'em.

In more detail we suggest the following talk plan format:

1. The attention grabber	Something that will make the audience sit up but is also relevant to your talk.
2. Common ground	Tell them about yourself, your experience, knowledge of the trade, mutual customers, contracts, etc.
3. Tell 'em what you're going to tell 'em	i.e. the purpose of this talk is to explain what I can (briefly) of the products/services, the strengths of my company/myself and the benefits to you.
4. Tell 'em in detail	Expand 3 above in detail and encourage questions.
5. Tell 'em what you've told 'em	Conclude your talk by reminding them that you have explained your products/services, why they should buy from you and the benefits to them.

| 6. <u>The next step</u> | Tell them what you want of them now, e.g. 'Thank you for your attention, and I would now like to sit down with your key people to progress this matter.' |

As we said at the beginning of this topic, giving presentations is not to everybody's taste. However, it is part of being self-employed and is the most powerful vehicle to get your ideas across, thereby facilitating your ability to sell your goods and services.

Three last tips:

- Remember the audience is usually sympathetic and on your side to begin with; keep it that way.
- Aim for, and explain, a win-win outcome.
- Learn to enjoy your time on your feet and, hopefully, become accomplished at giving powerful presentations.

Good luck!

Delegation

Delegation means handing over some of your work to somebody else, and is not restricted to organizations with more formal structures. It is just as essential for the self-employed person to delegate, otherwise you will end up doing all the work yourself and being so busy that you will be unable to grow the business. Delegation is the transfer of authority and responsibility to do the job to a third party but with you keeping the accountability, i.e. the buck stops with you.

Delegation can be to an employee, a colleague, a contractor, an agency person or to a machine, e.g. a computer to do your book-keeping. For the self-employed the prime purpose of delegation is to make time available in order to concentrate on priority and higher level work that will make a more significant contribution to your business. The following should where possible be delegated:

- Routine and repetitive tasks, because by their very nature you know all there is to know about them, making them easy to understand and therefore easier to explain and delegate.

- Tasks that you are not very good at. You cannot be good at everything so transfer the job to somebody better at it than you.
- Tasks that you do not like doing. Some cannot be delegated because they are your responsibility, e.g. dismissal of an employee. However, otherwise, if you don't like doing it, delegate.
- Tasks that you love doing. When you fall in love with a job, you will spend far too much time on it, and it will become unprofitable. Learn to let go and give the task away.

Delegation is a skill that can be learned through practice. The reasons that sometimes people are not very good at it are as follows:

- We have nobody trained up to do the job.
- We do not want to spend the money on another person.
- As perfectionists we take the view that nobody can do the job as quickly or as well as we can.
- We are control freaks – we do not trust the skill and abilities of other people and we prefer to keep everything under our control.

As we have said, in order to expand your business at some point delegation is essential. The following are guidelines on how to delegate:

- Plan your delegation well in advance, delegate the whole job – not just bits of it – and then only sizeable chunks of work.
- Clearly define what you want done, the reasons and the objectives of the job, and explain what authority you are giving the other person, including monetary responsibility, i.e. the budget.
- Agree target times for completion, and become hands off once the task has been delegated. Act as a coach, not a policeman.
- Give encouragement and praise a job well done.

Remember delegation is a very sound investment in your future and the future of your business.

Powerful and persuasive writing

A great deal of your work as a self-employed person may be through the written word. You will write letters to clients and customers asking for information, or agreement, or new work; you will send them information about yourself and your services or products; you will send out invoices and statements; you will correspond with a range of other suppliers, competitors, associates, etc.

Your writing will be a major 'shop window' for you. Many clients and customers will rarely meet with you – perhaps some never will, and they will only 'see' you through your letters and other written documents. Even in organizations where you make personal contact you may deal with other people you rarely or never meet. Therefore your writing must 'sell' you. Just as a shop dresses its window to show off its goods and its 'house style' to attract customers, and just as you dress yourself smartly for face to face meetings, so you must dress your writing to make a high impact.

The starting-point of writing

Start by thinking of the person you are writing to. Why are you writing to them? Is it to interest them in your services or product – in which case does your writing tell them what they need to know in clear, simple terms? Be sure you are telling them what *they* will find interesting or useful, not what *you* find interesting or useful. Write to *their* needs, not yours. Is it to state your position? In which case is it clearly stated, and is it stated in a way that takes regard of the reader's attitude?

Do you want them to respond in some way? In which case state clearly what you want of them.

Imagine your letter, invoice, sales brochure, etc. in the hands of the recipient. What does his or her face look like? Pleased? Enthusiastic? Puzzled? Bored? Whatever you imagine, ask yourself why.

Only when you know what impact you want to have and how you expect the reader to receive your document, can you design it effectively.

Keep your persuasive points to a minimum

It might seem to you that the more points you can present in favour of your argument the more effective your presentation will be. That is rarely the case. If you present twenty reasons to support your argument and one of them is weak it may be seized upon as a reason for not agreeing with you or complying with you. Five strong, unarguable points may have a greater impact. The shorter, punchier presentation is likely to be clearer, and have greater emphasis.

Synthesis

It is your job as writer to reduce the document to simple, readable and re-readable form. If you want to give someone three sentences it is far easier for them to give them the three sentences on a piece of paper than to point them at a floor to ceiling bookcase and tell them to find them for themselves. If you want them to read something, you do the work to point them to what you want them to read.

Exhibit enthusiasm

There is nothing so persuasive and infectious as enthusiasm. Let your excitement and involvement be obvious to others.

What's in it for them

Nothing interests readers more than seeing – preferably up front – what they stand to gain by going along with your message, complying with it or agreeing with it.

Nothing out of the blue; always 'out of the old'

You cannot present a new concept successfully without building it on a foundation of old and accepted knowledge that is familiar to the reader. People are simultaneously excited and threatened by change, so to play to that present them with the change (and the excitement) along with a foundation of the old (removing the threat of the unknown).

If you are offering clients an updated product, for example, first tell them how it will deal with the situations that the 'old version' deals with and for which they originally bought your earlier product. Then tell them about the enhancements.

Be specific

Vague terms usually hide something, and readers pick this up quickly. The more specific you can be, the more powerful your message will be. Telling someone that by accepting your proposals he or she will gain 'significant benefits' is not as clear as telling them they will save '£30,000 over the next three years'; the latter can be quantified and imagined. It can be compared to other alternatives. Precision inspires confidence and usefulness.

Use positive language

Be positive and optimistic in your use of language. If you must state a negative find the positive way to do so, thereby suggesting the solution rather than a problem. Instead of: 'We cannot process your order until we have your written confirmation' (problem), use: *'As soon as we have your written confirmation we will process your order' (solution).*

Sentence structure

Generally, for business writing use short and sharp sentences. Too many complex sentences can be tedious and time-consuming to read.

Use the sound bite mentality

Politicians and others making television appearances are advised to use sound bites – short, sharp, highly impactful statements – to put over their ideas. The same concept applies to business writing in the modern day. One tried and tested way to do this is to 'group' points into threes; known as triadic text. For example, from one newspaper report: 'When the miners were released by the rescuers, all were exhausted, some were in a state of shock and a few showed terrible signs of physical injury.' To try to express any more information about the miners in one sentence would become difficult to read, and of low impact.

Use active verbs

A verb is 'active' if the subject of the sentence is performing an action; the verb is 'passive' if the subject is receiving an action. For example, in the sentence 'The house was painted by Sean', because the house is the subject and is 'receiving' the painting, the verb is passive. On the other hand, in the sentence 'Sean painted the house', Sean is the subject and *doing* the painting so the verb is 'active' and has higher impact.

Keep to a neutral gender

Avoid gender-specific phrases such as 'The supervisor should consider his computer needs' (which implies masculine managers only). The same message can be put across without such impression being given by 'The supervisor should consider his or her computer needs' (reflecting both masculine and feminine) or 'Managers should consider their computer needs' (the plural pronoun is neutral in gender) or 'Managers must consider computer needs' (eliminating the pronoun altogether).

Ambiguity with dates

If you are writing to an audience where the date 'conventions' might be different, usually an international audience, then it is safest to spell out the month to ensure there is no error in understanding. For example, 6–9–99 would be interpreted in England as 6 September 1999 but in, say, America as 9 June 1999. Spelling out the month removes any doubt.

Editing and revision

The best writing requires editing, and plenty of it. To make the highest impact means that the thoughts you first wrote straight from your mind need careful crafting and manipulation to turn them into something impactful. Try to leave time between drafting and editing, giving yourself opportunity to come to it with a fresh mind. You cannot do the two things at the same time; writing is creative, editing is destructive and critical even if it is designed to lead to a creative finale.

Editing takes time and planning. Consider the phrase used by Winston Churchill when writing to President Roosevelt: 'I am sorry I had to write you a long letter as I did not have time to write you a short one.' What it means is that anyone can ramble; a short punchy presentation on paper needs care and attention.

Information technology

Business writing can be greatly enhanced with the application of modern technology: word processors, spell-checkers, computerized thesauri, electronic mail memos, graphics, all-in-one systems, etc. The drudgery of writing can be reduced or removed with technology capable of doing the basics, leaving you free to use your imagination and creativity.

The most common modern aid is the word processor, that function of a personal computer that has all but replaced the typewriter. Most word processors offer:

- A range of fonts (typestyles) and enhancements allowing the finished document to contain several different typefaces including italics, emboldened words, underlined words and many others.
- A 'cut and paste' facility that allows for great flexibility in designing the document, moving paragraphs from one area of a document to another almost instantaneously.
- Templates which contain the 'standard information' for your documents that do not have to be typed in every time you write that type of document. For example, many small businesses keep their invoice 'template' in the computer with almost all the data already stored. When an invoice is needed only the client's name and address, and the specific invoice details and amounts, need to be typed in.

The availability and ease of use of such equipment has allowed many small businesses to dispense with costly secretarial functions, and people at all levels in businesses often type their own work. Some small businesses have no 'standard' secretarial functions at all.

The last step
Arguably the most important part of any letter, report, brochure, etc. is the clear instruction to the reader as to 'what to do next'. Many good brochures and letters fall at the last hurdle because the reader, even if impressed by the writing, simply puts the document aside for later. Many believe that the letter or brochure is a fore-runner of your next follow up and downgrade it as such.

If you want the reader to telephone you, or place an order, or make an enquiry, or whatever, then say so clearly and boldly. End the letter with something like: 'If the proposals in this letter appeal to you then please telephone me at the above number to arrange a demonstration' or something akin to this. You might even be more specific; there is nothing like a deadline to concentrate the mind. 'Once you have read through this report please telephone me before Friday 7th, etc., to discuss it further.' If it is a brochure then make the final section the reader sees your name, address, telephone, fax number, e-mail address, etc. and a clear statement: 'What you should do now is contact us at the above to arrange a meeting.'

Debt management

Debts and debtors are a fact of life for most businesses. Normal commercial practice will probably force you to sell some goods or services 'on credit', waiting for a time for payment. Inevitably anything other than taking cash at the time of sale increases the risk of not being paid, either because of error, dispute, the financial collapse of the customer, or other sundry reasons.

Taking this risk is normal, and even losing a small percentage of debt to 'bad debts' is a fact of business life because it shows that the business is ready to take risks, which it must do. If a business takes 50 risks and loses one then it still has 49 gains it would not have had if it had played safe. But equally, a business can become too reckless, lending to obviously bad risks. Good debt management is the fine line between risk and recklessness.

But never be in doubt what you are doing: selling on credit is the equivalent of giving someone a loan. You should be as careful in giving that loan as you would be if someone asked you to loan them money out of your wallet. Because that in effect is what you are doing.

There are some very basic rules that can be put in place from the outset of your business to let you make the right judgements, and to minimize the risk of losing money.

Credit checks and references, and the use of credit limits

Before lending to anyone, particularly when lending a substantial amount, it is wise to take some references. Ask for the names of other businesses that have extended credit and follow up the names; write to them and ask for confirmation of good payment. Telephoning can also be useful here. Some people will tell you on the telephone what they might be reluctant to commit to writing. You might also consider the use of specialist credit reference agencies who use a variety of methods to compose a profile of the business and allocate it a 'credit risk rating'. These two procedures will minimize the risk of lending to obvious, or notorious, bad payers.

Remember to also use your own experience. If a business starts to become a bad payer, be quick to withdraw credit, and certainly do not extend it, unless you are satisfied that the reasons are acceptable.

If the sum being 'lent' is too small to merit the cost of such effort then take an intuitive guess and learn by your inevitable occasional mistakes. However, do not let a company 'sucker' you into lending more and more. Some less than honest businesses will ask for small credit amounts to be extended, pay very promptly, and gradually increase the demand for more credit. By now you think you have built up trust in them, and then suddenly they fail to pay a large amount they have persuaded you to extend. To avoid this make it a policy of your company to take references and use agencies whenever the amount of credit being sought exceeds a certain limit, a limit which you will have to judge based on your business. One obvious criterion in setting that limit is that it should be low enough so that occasional losses up to that figure will not overly harm your cashflow.

Invoices
The design of the invoice can be the first step to avoiding bad debts. A clear invoice with clear details setting out the terms of payment will make it harder for those wishing to avoid or delay payment to do so.

Ensure that your invoices have the following details, some of which are required by law, and others which are good business practice:

• The full name and trading address of your company. Also telephone, fax and e-mail numbers.
• The accounts department address, or address to which the remittance should be paid if different from that above.
• A named individual, perhaps you the proprietor, who should be contacted in case of dispute or query.
• If a limited company, then the registered office and the place and number of registration.
• The business's VAT number, if applicable.
• A prominent invoice number which can always be used as a reference in correspondence. It is preferable if that is also part

of an internal sequence that makes follow up in your own company easy.

- The tax point and date of invoice. These are often the same.
- A clear description of what the invoice is for, when goods were delivered, and any cross reference to the customer's own documentation, e.g. purchase order.
- A due date by which it is payable. Do not say 'thirty days' or something like this as it is an unclear 'target' in the mind of the receiver. Spell out the exact date on which payment is due; it becomes a focus for the payer.
- The calculation of VAT and the amount of VAT applicable.

You might increase ease of payment if you do some of the customer's work for him or her. For example, your customer needs to keep the invoice in the business records but also needs something to pay your cheque with. Consider providing a two-piece invoice, the copy to be sent back to you as a remittance advice. Alternatively have a tear off strip to attach to the cheque. If you really want to be helpful design it so that your address is in the right place for a 'window envelope'.

Be efficient and project your efficiency – this will be the first warning to slow payers that you will see what they are doing and will chase them vigorously. Send out your invoice as soon as practicable. If you do not invoice for six months you not only increase the risk of loss due to error, dispute and financial collapse but you are signalling the payer that you are inefficient and will probably take another six months to realize you have not received payment.

Statements

The regular issuing of statements keeps the issue of payment to you fresh in the mind of the debtor. To keep costs to a minimum you might decide to send statements only to those you know are slow payers or to anyone whose balance exceeds a certain period of time. Statements should contain the same basic information as the invoices, should detail the amounts outstanding fully and not just as 'brought forward balances', and provide for an easy means of using the statement as a way of paying the bill. Using brightly coloured 'overdue' stickers available from stationers can be an effective extra reminder to late payers.

Never use expressions like 'First Reminder' – it suggests that there will be others and that therefore this 'first' reminder can be safely ignored.

Charging interest to debtors

You may decide to charge interest on debts outstanding to defray your own costs of running credit and to encourage debtors to pay more promptly. Until recently you may only legally have done so if you made this clear at the time when the contract for sale was made, otherwise you were not able to charge interest.

However, at the time of writing the law relating to this is changing, with the provisions affecting small businesses already in force.

The Late Payment of Commercial Debts (Interest) Act 1998 brings into effect the government's commitment to a statutory right for businesses to charge interest on the late payment of commercial debts. It was a subject much discussed, but never dealt with, by the previous Conservative administration, but was one of the first actions of the new Labour administration of 1997. The government published a Green Paper *Improving the Payment Culture* on 28 July 1997 and received overwhelming response, mostly positive, from the business community. The purpose of the legislation was to ensure that the cost of delaying payment of debt was borne by the individuals who controlled the dates of payment, i.e. the customer or client rather than the seller.

Because it was perceived that the smaller businesses were those at the mercy of larger corporations the Act, which will phase in the full legislation in three stages, first addressed those smaller enterprises.

The introduction of the Act will be as follows:

1. On 1 November 1998 small businesses will be able to apply the provisions of the Act against large businesses and public sector organizations.
2. After a period, expected to be two years, the Act will be broadened to allow small businesses to use the legislation against all other businesses and the public sector.
3. Finally, after a further two years, the right will be extended universally, with all enterprises able to enforce the Act against all other enterprises.

To prevent large corporations using their 'muscle' to demand unfair terms of repayment and interest rates and thereby effectively getting round the Act 'through the back door' the Act has provisions to test the terms of any contract for 'reasonableness' and to set aside any terms thought to be unreasonable. Guidelines for this are probably indicated by the 'default' terms given in the Act for payment periods and interest rates. They state that the 'default' period will be 30 days outstanding, and that the interest rate is likely to be base rate plus 8 per cent, but subject to change. There is no minimum size of debt under the Act.

A small business for this purpose is defined as having 50 or less full-time employees, or part-time equivalents.

To make a claim the supplier should inform the purchaser in writing that interest will be sought. The letter should indicate how much is owed, showing debt and interest separately, and what the debt is for, itemizing specific supplies. It should state to whom payment should be made, and at what address, and indicate what payment method is acceptable. Claimants do not have to make a claim immediately; a claimant has six years to make a claim (five years in Scotland).

But small firms remain concerned that they will upset their larger customers if they enforce these rules. In the *Financial Mail on Sunday* of 11 October 1998 several such fears were voiced. For example, Dr Bernard Juby of the Federation of Small Businesses commented that 'large firms will simply threaten to take their business elsewhere'.

However, the overriding belief is that even if the legislation does not change matters overnight it will lead to a culture where delayed payment is less acceptable. The long-term effect could be successful in the end.

Factoring

One way to relieve the several burdens of debt collection and debtors is to factor debts. A factoring agency – usually an arm of the major banks – takes over the management of your debt and pays you more quickly than you are likely to achieve, thereby accelerating your cashflow. For this you pay a percentage of the amounts involved as a fee. But note that you do not acquire any bad debt relief from this as any debts unrecovered are still charged back to you. The process is one of cashflow (timing) relief only.

Your customers are told to pay their cheques directly to the factoring agency, and for this reason factoring has in the past given the impression of a business in trouble, needing outside help and so on. In the past, factoring has also been very expensive and therefore *has* in fact tended to be used by companies in trouble. The climate is at present changing to one more like that in the United States where factoring is common and without stigma. The rates are generally lower than they have been and the importance of cashflow is more widely accepted and understood, and it is highly likely that factoring will be more commonly applied in the future. (The introduction of *The Late Payment of Commercial Debts (Interest) Act 1998* may affect that position to some extent, but it is as yet too soon to know in what way.)

One other advantage of factoring that small businesses acquire is that debt collection and chasing is put in the hands of professionals who have time and expertise to do it, and who can pursue more intransigent payers vigorously but without breaking laws which are, in general, frankly angled in favour of the debtor rather than the seller.

'Recovery' letters

If you do choose to maintain your own debt control and do your own debt chasing then the key to effective pursuit of intransigent payers is often in the impact of the 'recovery' letter sent when statements appear to have had no effect.

The letter should be blunt without being rude, and should stick very much to the point, ignoring any diversions that might have been offered to you. For example, if the proprietor of a business tells you that he or she has been unable to pay you because they have had difficulties in their personal life do not refer to those difficulties in your recovery letter; they are not your problem and they blur the issue, as they were probably intended to do.

Use short, clear sentences. Explain what is outstanding, what exactly you are demanding, and when payment should be made (*now!* presumably). Never apologize for asking for your money; if anything you are due an apology, not due to offer one. Do not ask for less than the full sum or you will literally, and stupidly, have asked for exactly what you will probably get – less. Do not ask why you have not been paid; your lack of enquiry will show that this is irrelevant. The point is that you want paying now. You may wish to set out your next recovery steps if payment is not received, e.g. application to a court. If you do threaten such action always be ready to carry it through or your debtor will sense your lack of resolve and you will have made matters worse. Stress the positive, that you have enjoyed a good relationship which you value and that the late payment is causing a deterioration which you regret, and that payment will rectify that deterioration.

Never let the letter look like a 'form' letter routinely sent out; it will weaken its impact. Use the company name and individual names and references to show that this letter has been especially tailored. Refer to any previous correspondences to show that you have your eye on this matter very closely.

The Small Claims Court

If the suggestions referred to above are followed then you will reduce to a minimum the number of debts where payment is avoided, or that become bad, or need legal action taken. However, legal action is bound to arise in a small number of debts and for small businesses many of their debts will fall into a category that can be dealt with through the Small Claims Court.

This is a very effective way of winning a case, but be aware that winning does not mean you will be paid your money. Many actions are not defended and you win by default, but you may only have the 'pleasure' of attaching a County Court Judgement to the debtor, affecting his ability to get credit in the future – you may not get paid. Enforcement is a separate procedure and frankly the court's bailiffs are often about as effective as a chocolate teapot. Private bailiffs may be more effective, but this costs more money and you are still not guaranteed a recovery of the sums due.

The smaller debts go to arbitration (larger debts can if both parties agree), which is less strict than a formal court hearing but which is still a very formal procedure. The advantage is that minimal court costs and small sundry costs are all that are incurred, and solicitors are not used, thereby cutting down legal fees.

The process is that you will prepare a submission to the court setting out what you are owed and why, and what steps you have already taken for recovery. You complete this on a pro-forma provided by the court, and you submit copies for the court and each defendant. The court then delivers this to the defendant who has a fixed period of time for a response.

The defendant may agree to pay but ask for additional time, offering the court details of his or her financial situation. You may accept this, but if you do not then the registrar taking the case will seek to find agreeable terms. If you believe the debtor has been dishonest in stating his or her financial position then you should bring your evidence to the registrar.

If the action is to be defended then it will be moved to the court dealing with the address of the defendant; one example of the process being weighted in favour of the debtor and against you. The court issues you with a plaint number, which is a reference for your case to be used whenever you write to the court.

You will submit the full details of your claim to the registrar, with a copy also delivered to the defendant. The defendant will then submit his or her defence to the registrar. Then a hearing date will be set for the registrar to question both parties and come to a decision.

Precise procedures during the hearing vary somewhat from registrar to registrar but generally, both sides having submitted their written representations, the registrar will first establish at the hearing the terms of the claim, then question both sides to agree the facts. To avoid fruitless argument between the parties the registrar will usually insist on the parties responding to him or her and not debating amongst themselves. In most cases the registrar will come to a decision then and there.

Bookkeeping

This is the process of keeping a financial record of the business. It gives you understanding of your business, and complies with legal – basically tax and public filing – legislation.

What to record

Exactly how you will keep your records and what records you should keep will depend to some extent on the type of business you are in. However, there are some basic rules.

You need to record your income and be able to prove that income to the tax authorities with as much documentation as reasonably possible. If you invoice your customers and clients, then keep copies of the invoices. These should be summarized in two ways: a listing of the invoices raised to each individual customer (the Sales Ledger) and a listing of the total amount of invoices raised each day, or week, or month (the Sales Day Book). The former, adjusted by the amounts you have been paid from your customers, will enable you to collate your debts outstanding from others (debtors), broken down into each individual debtor. The latter will enable you to know how much you have made from sales over a period.

Some businesses do not raise invoices – shops for example – so to keep the equivalent of a Sales Day Book they must retain till rolls, details of paying-in to the bank, and so on. They do not generally need a Sales Ledger of course as they receive cash at the time, though some shops keep accounts for certain customers, an unreconciled Sales Ledger, for those few people.

You should also keep the 'Purchase' equivalents of the Sales books – a Purchase Ledger and a Purchase Day Book, relating to your trade purchases, i.e. the stock you buy for resale or other direct costs. The former will record who you have bought from on credit and therefore owe money to, and – set against payments made – will enable you to know at any point how much you owe to others, and to whom it is owed. The Day Book records the amounts spent periodically on these direct costs.

You must also keep a record of other expenses, and it is helpful to keep that record with some basic analysis. Instead of recording only how much was spent on the business each day, or week, or month, it is useful to keep a breakdown of major expenses. For each period the expenditure should be broken down into, say, motor expenses, travel and accommodation, wages and subcontracted work, general administration such as stationery and telephone, office costs such as rent and rates, and a variety of other headings dependent on the detail of the business in question. These are maintained in what is traditionally known as a Nominal Ledger.

You will record the actual payments in one, and possibly two, books. A Cash Book refers usually to what is paid in and spent from the bank and is a mirror image of the bank statements. Actual cash is recorded through a Petty Cash Book.

If you pay wages then you are required to keep a record of what you have paid to each individual and what deductions you have made from their wages for tax and National Insurance, and a record of those deductions being paid over to the tax authorities.

You will also need to record what money you have personally taken from the business, either as salary in the case of a Limited Company or drawings in the case of a sole trader or partnership. If you introduce money into the business, that must also be recorded.

For those businesses that keep stocks you need some system of recording not just the purchases (noted above) but also the usages and wastages. Periodically you should perform physical stock-takes to check actual stock against what your records say. This will correct errors, and is a security against theft within your own business.

As a matter of good discipline it is generally advisable to keep as low a level of stocks as possible. Money tied up in stock is not earning interest, is not available for other uses, and is not easily turned into cash. Furthermore stockholding costs money: for storage, for maintenance, for security, and so on. You should set your stock level at the lowest possible amount commensurate with having enough to fulfil an expected level of ordering or manufacture, with perhaps a buffer to allow for unusual orders, or problems in supply from your suppliers. The only valid reason for high stock levels would be buying in bulk cheaply – perhaps acquiring stocks from a supplier in liquidation.

You must also keep other records. Your bank statements are evidence of money banked and spent, and they should be reconciled (i.e. agreed) to your Cash Book periodically and never less frequently than monthly. This means checking what you think you paid in and out of the bank against the statements and adjusting for any errors. Keep also your cheque stubs, and paying-in book stubs. The actual cash in hand – in the petty cash box, for example – should be periodically reconciled to the Petty Cash Book.

You sometimes need to keep special records. For example if you take goods for personal use from your stocks, you need to record this to comply with both Inland Revenue and VAT legislation.

How to keep the records

The choice of storage medium for your records is varied, with an increasing emphasis on computerized systems. The cost of such systems has reduced so much in recent years that it is rarely a deciding factor any more. Computer-literacy is now the main criterion, and systems are addressing that by becoming much more 'user-friendly' than ever before.

One system is to keep a set of separate books along the lines discussed above: Sales Ledger, Sales Day Book, Purchase Ledger, Purchase Day Book, Nominal Ledger, Cash Book and Petty Cash Book. For the larger or more complex business, this is possibly necessary – particularly if you have large numbers of customers and suppliers so you need to keep a track of debtors and creditors in detail.

But for smaller businesses, or those with uncomplicated needs, there are many 'all-in-one' books available. They have several sets of pages throughout and the book is designed to last for one year. There are weekly or monthly pages to record bank and cash movements (replacing the Cash Book and the Petty Cash Book), pages to record sales per day, week, or month, replacing the Sales Day Book, and pages to record purchases replacing both the Purchase Day Book and the Nominal Ledger. The 'sales' and 'purchases' sections have a 'date paid' column which allows you to see who owes and is owed; a very basic form of sales and purchases ledger. The book also allows for the extraction of VAT, which would normally be done in the individual books, and has special sheets to record each VAT quarter's figures to tie up with the forms sent to the VAT Office.

But it is to computers that most people are turning. The time is approaching, it would seem, when every household will have a PC. Even those purchased to provide children with schoolwork reference, or as a games machine, usually have a package of software including word processor (which has all but replaced the typewriter) and spreadsheets.

Spreadsheets can be very easily designed to produce the pages of the books mentioned above in computerized form so that the same information can be stored on computer. The spreadsheets also remove much of the calculation. The input is fitted into a 'template' and the computer does the tedious adding up.

Also becoming very economical are the software packages designed to provide full double-entry bookkeeping that complies with all the requirements of the law and which, in theory at least, are adequate to maintain the records of even the largest companies. Yet they are available for no more than a few hundred pounds – sometimes less – from the high street. These systems simplify data entry, and eliminate arithmetic errors. For example, by entering one sales invoice the computer automatically updates both the Sales Day Book and the Sales Ledger. By entering the receipt of a sum from a debtor the computer automatically updates both the bank account and the Sales Ledger. It completes the double-entry with each single input, saving time and reducing error. (Double-entry is the accountancy term which recognizes that each transaction has an equal and opposite effect in the books, and provides for control checks to see that the records are being maintained correctly.)

Although there are a number of packages available the two that we have found most commonly in use with small businesses are Sage and Quickbooks.

Sage has several 'levels' depending on the degree of sophistication required, including some which maintain stock control. The newest versions are easy to input to, and provide clear output. They come with relatively easy to read manuals, on-screen help facilities and, though quite expensive, a support line with knowledgeable people who can answer questions when you can't work out what to do.

All of that is similarly available with Quickbooks which we have found equally popular. It is extremely user-friendly. One of the main advantages is that the accounts can be built 'as you go' rather than needing to be tailored at the beginning. If you want to include new lines of sales or purchases, etc. you simply add them at the moment of data entry and the computer re-designs the output seamlessly. Output is also extraordinarily clear, in both alphanumeric form or graph form in highly colourful, easy-to-understand graphs.

No doubt as time goes on these and other packages will be refined still further, and it can only be a short time before every business maintains its records on some sort of computerized system.

When to keep the records
The one habit to avoid is putting all the year's records together one day ready to see your accountant the next day! That said,

most accountants have a few clients who do just that. The drawbacks are obvious:

- You will lose receipts during the year and therefore not claim legitimate expenses against your income.
- You may lose track of your income and could be breaking the law by submitting erroneous accounts.
- You will forget what certain receipts were for, or forget other information, and enter it wrongly or not at all.
- Most importantly, you will not have a 'feel' for your business throughout the year, and you will not be properly in control of cash, of debtors, of payments. You will not know if you are profitable, or how much you can or cannot take as personal drawings. In fact you will only succeed despite yourself, if in fact you do succeed.

Writing up the books – manually or on computer – should be a frequent and regular habit. The pace of some businesses dictates that this be done daily, or weekly, or monthly. Whatever the requirement, we would suggest never less than monthly. VAT registered businesses usually have to return figures quarterly but even then they should be more frequently maintained than that.

In addition, reconciliations should be done monthly. That means checking the bank statements from the bank against your Cash Book to ensure that if you have made errors they are found and corrected sooner rather than later. It means checking what you think you are owed according to your Sales Ledger against the total sales for the period less the total receipts from debtors in the period; the overall figure should be the same as the addition of the individual debtor balances. Similarly for purchases.

How to acquire the skills
Accountants generally accept that about half of the bookkeeping they do for clients is for those who cannot do it for themselves, and the other half for clients who, while technically able, are too busy and make better use of their time selling, or consulting, or whatever it is they do for their clients and customers. So the first question is to decide whether or not you want to do any book-keeping, or whether you would rather pay an accountant or bookkeeper to do it for you.

But you might well decide that doing your own bookkeeping is a discipline which keeps you in touch with the administration of your own business. For that, or other reasons, you might decide to do it yourself. If you do, then you will probably benefit from an appointment with your accountant to discuss the system that will be most suitable for you. We would not suggest attending evening classes or special courses in bookkeeping. These are generally for those who will become bookkeepers and who need to be flexible to deal with a number of client systems. They are generally too complicated for one individual system.

We would suggest the following is a good starter routine for most small businesses:

- Discuss the system that would suit you with your accountant.
- Have your accountant set up the system with you, whether manually or on computer.
- Input the first month's data yourself, then take it back to your accountant to check. He or she can then explain where you are going wrong.
- Continue to do the next few months, perhaps calling your accountant when you are really lost on certain 'one-off' items.
- Make an appointment after a period of a few months – and often at the time of the first VAT period-end when the VAT return needs to be completed. Have the accountant check the records again, correct any errors, and assist you in pulling out the VAT figures.
- Then do the next VAT quarter entirely yourself, but get your accountant to check your workings.
- After this you should be ready to fly solo. If you find real problems your accountant is still there to help, but probably any errors that do occur will not distort the figures too much and will be picked up at the year-end accounts preparation.

The use of technology

Businesses need certain technologies to survive. It is hard to imagine anyone running a business in the modern day without the use of a telephone, for example. But the mobile phone revolution is such that these devices have made many changes to even this simple communication. Secretaries have become less necessary for smaller businesses thanks to the ability to take and make calls from anywhere on a mobile. Most mobiles also have an inbuilt voicemail facility allowing the user to switch off the phone for important meetings and then later retrieve messages while still away from the office.

The use of fax is now pretty much universal. There was a time when people stopped asking if you had a fax and just asked for your fax number. Anyone without a fax was viewed as somewhat behind the times.

The IT (information technology) revolution is such that it is hard to imagine trying to run any reasonable size of business – and certainly any service profession – without the use of a computer for at least some function. Bookkeeping and accountancy have already been considered. The use of word processor software, replacing typewriters, is now firmly established. Many computers now also have software that replaces the need for a separate fax and even an answering machine.

But there are also functions that have been created specifically by the computer, and for which the computer is the only means of application, in particular the increasingly popular use of e-mail. The point has rapidly been reached as with fax of years ago when people ask only what your e-mail address is rather than if you have one.

E-mail is an incredibly useful tool for modern business. It is a means of electronically transferring information from one computer to another anywhere in the world. The size of the transfer is almost unlimited – we have transferred whole book manuscripts from computer to computer in just minutes. The system works by preparing a document, or any number of documents, for transfer, then using a modem to link your computer to a telephone line, then transferring the document, and then 'hanging up' the telephone line. The transfer calls are usually at local, and therefore relatively cheap, rates. You do not have to deal with items one at a time; the general procedure is to 'log on', i.e. connect up the telephone line periodically, download all the messages and information that have been sent to you from people all around the world, then 'hang up', deal with all your replies, and then 'connect' again just to transmit your electronic post. In addition to words, the e-mail will allow for the transfer of photographs (though you would need a 'scanner' to originate them), or of whole accounts packages. We have clients who transfer their whole year's accounts through e-mail to our computers where we can process them. We then send back the processed information and the only time there is a paper-print taken is for legal signature purposes. Even transferring information to the Inland Revenue can be done by accountants through a form of e-mail.

Along with e-mail usually comes the availability to access the Internet, or World Wide Web. This is a system, not owned or controlled by anyone or by a government, which allows all computers to display and read information from businesses and individuals all around the world. For getting trade and professional information from anywhere in the world there is no more efficient method, and it is rapidly becoming an essential tool of small businesses.

It is also possible to 'build your own website'. This means that you can put the equivalent of a brochure and contact details onto the Internet where anyone in the world can read it and contact you for your services. The system also allows for 'hyperlinks' to other sites so that for example several businesses may create 'links' to each other, allowing those accessing them to quickly switch between sites. For example, if you are a solicitor with a website you may create a link to your friendly local accountant, who has a reciprocal link to your site. Anyone accessing either site sees that with a click of their computer mouse they can then go straight to a complementary site for further services.

There are classes and courses available to learn about getting the best from these technologies, and there are specialist services who can build websites and offer other advice.

The alternative method favoured by many entrepreneurs is to get their teenage children to teach them!

Networking

Local and national business events provide an opportunity to get your business on other people's agendas, to let them know what you can do for them. But networking is fraught with difficulties and often the only tangible product of a business event is a stomach full of wine and sandwich-quarters.

It doesn't have to be that way. The following tips help to make the day useful, and pleasant:

- *Get ready ahead of time*. What other businesses will be there? Which ones do you want to target? What have you got to offer them? Have ready your leaflets, brochures and business cards – and ensure you are familiar with their content – so that you can point out to other delegates the bits that will be of interest to them rather than to you.

- *Make a good impression*. Okay, let's wheel out the old cliché for another airing: 'You never get a second chance to make a first impression'. At networking events this is as true as it ever will be. Total strangers who either will or will not ring you tomorrow can only judge you by your literature, your appearance and your attitude. Dress appropriately, act authoritatively and assertively. Be what you want them to think you are. 'Success breeds success' states another adage. Look successful if you want people to believe you are; and you *do* want them to believe you are successful – people don't pay money to those who look as if they've failed already.

- *Remember why you're there*. Small talk about the weather and your golf handicap might be a good ice-breaker but you're not there to improve your handicap, you're there to improve your business. So talk business. It is not rude; remember that the other people are there to talk business too. They expect it, and they want to as well.

- *Be a good listener*. Learn something, and make sure that others believe you have taken an interest in them. If they mention their sons' and daughters' names, remember them and drop them back into the conversation somewhere, or wish them well by name when the two of you part company and move on to talk to others.

- *Don't think you should talk about business to men, and cooking and the children to women*. Women certainly will be turned off. They're there for business too and the modern pressures of society unfortunately mean that they have to prove it more than men do. In any case, you'll find with experience that it is generally men who talk about the children at those sorts of events if anyone does.

- *Ask questions, and answer them*. People are probing each other, trying to find out how they would work together on a longer-term basis. The object of the event is not just to get rid of as many business cards as possible, but to do so in a memorable and useful way to people who will do more than throw them in the waste-basket by the taxi-rank outside. And asking questions shows an interest.

- *Work your suit or handbag.* You won't find it possible to carry a briefcase of literature around with you, talk, drink wine and eat vol-au-vents at the same time. The briefcase will have to go. Designate two pockets in your suit, or compartments in your shoulder bag, for business cards; one for you to give out, and one for others you get. Ensure that you ask for one from those you give one to. This serves two purposes; it shows you are as interested in them and what they have to offer as you want them to be in you, and it means you can send everyone you gave a card to a note the following day thanking them for their conversation the night before and reminding them about you.

- *Have a notepad and pen to hand.* On the notepad make notes of things you want to show you are particularly interested in while talking to people, and follow up in writing the next morning. On the business cards you receive – after you have gained a moment alone away from the person you were speaking to and before you get to the next one – jot personal notes, hobby interests, names of children, etc. – so that you can mention them in passing in your note the next day. Don't make those notes in front of the person.

- *Keep your briefcase with little else in it but your literature* somewhere available so that if your conversation really leads to it being appropriate you can offer the literature then and there. But don't press it; better really to post it along the next day. For two reasons: it gives you a reason for a follow-up. And the other person has wine and vol-au-vents to deal with as well!

- *Get round the room.* Too often people find a person to talk to and park themselves with them for the duration rather than make the effort of meeting others. It's a waste of time; yours and theirs. You are there to get round and meet other business people. So get moving. Make excuses like having to go get some food and drink, or be straight with them and admit you want to get round the room; the other person should agree with you and if they don't you have given them a free and valuable lesson in what they are there for too!

- *Have fun.* Don't go round the room looking like you're attending a business event! Go round looking like you're at ease in this, your natural environment. Comfortable people are easy to get on with, and experienced people are easy to deal with. Look comfortable and experienced and people will seek you out if they are having a hard time.

And you might just come away well-fed, well-networked – and smiling.

5 / What Type of Business Do I Want?

People starting up on their own, or with partners, need to decide what type of business organizations are available to them and what is the most suitable for their type of operation and circumstances. In this chapter we shall examine the choices available together with the advantages and disadvantages of each. Most people starting their own business are bombarded with advice from friends and acquaintances who are self-employed, as well as from professional advisors such as bankers, solicitors and accountants, and in coming to any decision must consider criteria such as simplicity, formation costs, legal obligations, risk and status. Traditionally most people start off as a sole trader and then evolve into either a partnership or a limited company. Let us consider the various types of business form and evaluate the use of them.

Sole trader

The most common form of self-employment is the sole trader. As the name indicates, you are on your own, and the management risks and rewards of the business are all yours. Being a sole trader is the simplest form of business organization, and attracts very little in start-up costs. All that is necessary is for you to decide a trading name, often your own name or your name together with your trade, e.g. J. Smith (Carpenter), and then to use that name for your letterheads, invoices, order pads, etc., and also to set up your bank account and register with the appropriate authorities, such as the Inland Revenue.

If you wish you can carry on business under a name which is

not your own name; there is no provision in law for registration, however there are restraints on name usage which will be discussed later when we look at limited companies. For some reason sole traders seem to lack the status of a limited company. Many people still associate limited companies with respectability and in our experience if you wish to raise finance as a sole trader, investors and lenders may be put off by the sole-trader entity. Indeed, it would seem that most investors and lenders are quite irrational in this context, as sole traders have unlimited liability to creditors, whereas limited liability companies protect the owners.

Sole practitioner

A sole practitioner is a professionally qualified sole trader, i.e. accountant, solicitor, dentist, architect, independent financial advisor, and so on. The only difference between a sole trader and practitioner is that the latter has to conduct business within the rules and regulations of their governing bodies, which often places stricter obligations on the individual than are applicable to sole traders.

Partnerships

If two or more people want to set up in business together or, say, two sole traders want to merge their businesses, the most popular path is to form a partnership. Similar to sole traders, partnerships have unlimited liability, and the partners are responsible for all profits and losses. Partnerships are a very flexible way to conduct business, enjoying all the benefits of being self-employed but sharing the management, risk and success with chosen colleagues.

In a partnership the partners have to decide how the business is to be managed, and how to divide profits and losses and other areas of responsibility. Although it is still not that common for small partnerships, it is advisable to draw up and enter into a partnership agreement. Obviously accountants, banks and solicitors can advise here but in order to save time, and costs it is advisable to at least settle the main heads of agreement as to how the partnership is to be conducted. The following guidelines are intended as a starting-point for discussions leading to agreement which can then be written up into a partnership agreement with the help of your professional advisor.

Name

The trading name of a partnership usually reflects the names of the founding partners, or their initials only, together with a brief description of which trade or profession they are in. There are some restrictions as to what name you can use and the rules for partnerships are similar to the rules governing limited companies which will be discussed later in this chapter.

Share of profits and losses

From our experience it is essential to establish right at the outset the formula for the calculation of profits and losses and division of such. In a simple partnership it may be sufficient to agree to divide up profits and losses equally. However, most partnerships prefer to establish a formula based on such criteria as number of days worked in a year, fees billed to customers and clients by each partner, number of customers and clients introduced by partners, and adjustments for such matters as bad debts, etc. Of course any such division of profits and losses can be altered with the agreement of all partners.

Salaries

Some partnership agreements stipulate that some partners will draw a set salary before any division of profits or losses. These salaried partners are often not true partners but rather like employees except that they have been awarded the status of being called a partner and often they will become true profit-sharing partners in due course.

Capital and loans introduced

Partners need to agree what capital and loans, and in what form, i.e. money and/or other assets, they are going to introduce to the partnership. It will also be necessary to agree if capital and loans introduced bear interest, at what rate (e.g. linked to the bank rate) and the repayment terms.

Domestic arrangements

At the start of the partnership it is sensible to agree internal domestic arrangements, both financial and non-financial. Financial matters may include arrangements for signing the cheques, expense accounts, authorization of revenue and capital limits, and the value of motor cars partners can purchase (if any) with partnership monies. Non-financial issues may cover holiday arrangements and any other domestic matters that come to mind.

Retirement and exit routes
Although it may seem a strange thing to do so early, it is advisable at the beginning of the partnership to agree what happens when a partner resigns or wants to retire. A retiring partner with a large amount of capital in the partnership could cause the other partners problems if the capital were to be taken out in one tranche. Partners need to agree how these situations are to be managed.

New partners
The partnership agreement should set out the terms and conditions whereby a new partner can be admitted to the partnership. Some firms try to match the timing of the arriving new partner with the exiting of an existing partner. If the new partner is required under the partnership agreement to introduce capital, then that capital may be used to pay out the retiring partner.

Management of the partnership
In small partnerships the management of the business is usually divided up by mutual consent based on the partners' experience and skill base, e.g. the partner with accounts experience and/or training will keep the books of accounts, whereas the partner with sales and marketing exposure will develop the customer client base. Larger partnerships may appoint a managing partner who is similar in role to the managing director of a limited company. In all cases who does what is a matter for the partners to decide, preferably at the outset.

Partner relations
Partnerships are very similar to close relationships, even to marriages, and they can turn sour for a variety of reasons. Therefore a well thought out and written partnership agreement is to be recommended. It has, frankly, been our experience, from a great many partnerships we have been able to study at close quarters,

that partnerships suffer a great deal of strain which often causes them to 'fracture'.

A partnership which consists of two similar people of similar skills may be very limiting in that the opportunity is missed to create synergy from two unalike people with different skill bases. Two decorators, for example, still have no marketing or selling expert which could make a big difference to getting good work. On the other hand if the partnership consists of a salesperson and a decorator there often comes a time when each thinks they are more important to the partnership than the other; when each thinks the other is not 'pulling their weight' as much. Arguments form over who should have the bigger share of the profits, or some other perk (the decorator needs a van, the salesperson 'needs' a Ferrari! – that sort of thing).

We examined one partnership which created artwork for magazines; one person was the creative side and the other the administrator. Both believed they were indispensable, both decided to go their separate ways; neither succeeded in their chosen fields and both ended up in employment.

In our experience further pressure also comes from the domestic partners of the pair – wives and husbands pressurizing the business partners in respect of profit share and perks.

The result is often that partnerships fracture after about three years and either evolve into sole traderships, or one partner leaves and is replaced by another.

In our experience partnerships with husbands and wives (or other domestic relationships) don't fare much better – the 'marriage' just goes with the business collapse.

Limited company

In the UK it is relatively easy to form a limited company. For less than a couple of hundred pounds you can purchase a ready-made company 'off the shelf' from company formation agents, or get your solicitor or accountant to form one for you.

The great advantage of limited companies is that if things should go wrong, then so long as you have traded within the law, you are protected from claims from your investors and creditors.

Limited companies are formed and regulated within the Companies Acts. The owners of the company called shareholders are liable for the debts of the company only up to the amount that they have agreed to pay for their shares in the company. As in nearly all cases these days shares are issued as fully paid. This means that in reality the shareholders stand to lose only what they have already invested. As previously mentioned, limited companies do seem to have more status than sole traders, although this is questionable considering the lack of personal risk often involved with limited companies.

Similar to when forming a partnership, when forming a limited company some decisions need to be taken up front and the following should assist the reader when starting or converting an existing business into a limited company.

How to form a limited company

There are two main ways to purchase your own limited company. One is to buy a ready-made company which has not traded, off the shelf, from company formation agents. These can be found in the telephone directory under that heading. As ready-made companies will have been formed with an existing name, you may of course keep that name or change it to what you wish if permission is granted. There is a cost involved in changing the name of a limited company so you may be advised to take the second option which is to have the formation agents, or your accountant or solicitor, form a company from scratch for you in the name of your choosing.

Some people need a company very quickly, perhaps to sign a contract or an agreement, in which case the 'off the shelf' route may be essential.

Name

Unlike a sole trader and partnership a limited company cannot necessarily trade using your name. The Registrar of Companies withholds the granting of a name if the name is already in use, is too like an existing name, or would give a wrong impression, e.g. for a £100 capitalized company to call itself Global or International. Certain other names are protected, such as those referring to the Crown, or government departments.

You do not have to trade in your company name (the 'limited' name) though you must display it on your letter headings. You may have a company called XYZ Ltd which trades as, say,

'Venture Printing'. However, banking regulations usually require cheques to the company to be made out to the 'limited' name.

Shareholders

A limited company is owned by its shareholders. Recent legislation makes it acceptable for there to be one shareholder only owning all of the shares. Shareholders, as owners of the company, are entitled to the profits which are distributed by way of dividends. (In small family companies the shareholder(s) may also be director(s) and they may take out some of their money through a salary which is a cost deductible in arriving at profit.)

Shareholders are only liable for the debts of the company up to that part of the shares that have not yet been paid for. Shareholders can vote at company meetings, and elect the directors who in turn run the company on behalf of the shareholders. For self-employed people using a limited company for a vehicle to trade this is somewhat academic, as normally they are a controlling director, i.e. owning the majority or all of the shares.

Under UK law there are private limited companies and public limited companies. The main differences between a private limited company and a public limited company are as follows:

- A private limited company has 'Limited' at the end of its name.
- A public limited company has 'Plc' at the end of its name.
- A private limited company can have one director only.
- A public limited company must have two or more directors.
- Only a 'Plc' may offer its shares to the public.
- A private limited company can start trading as soon as it is formed (incorporated).
- A 'Plc' must obtain a trading certificate from the Registrar of Companies.

All limited companies are governed by the Companies Acts, and by an internally generated set of 'rules' known as the Memorandum and Articles of Association.

Memorandum of Association

The Memorandum of Association sets out the following:

- The name of the company
- The registered office of the company
- The company's objects (activities and purposes)
- That the liability of the members is limited
- The authorized share capital of the company (the capital that *can* be issued, whether or not it has been)

Normally the objects of the company set out the prime purpose of the business (e.g. to carry on business as importers and exporters of jewellery), and then expanded objects give the company powers to do other things in order to fulfil the prime objects (e.g. to manufacture jewellery, etc.).

The authorized share capital is the amount of money that can be raised by selling shares to third parties.

Shareholders in meeting can alter the terms of the Memorandum of Association.

Articles of Association

If the Memorandum of Association sets out what the company is all about, the Articles of Association set out the rules and provisions relating to its corporate governance. In the Articles of Association are the provisions relating to the issue of shares, General Meetings and Resolutions, appointment and retirement of directors, and borrowing powers. If you purchase a company off the shelf you will be given a standard set of articles (which can be altered by a majority of shareholders in a meeting called for that purpose). For a large 'Plc' the articles can be quite extensive; for example, the revised Articles of Association of Railtrack Group Plc adopted with effect from 24 July 1997 ran to nearly 100 pages.

Summary

	Advantages	**Disadvantages**
Sole Trader and Sole Practitioner	Simple to set up. No start up costs. Little restriction on name usage. Financial information not publicly published.	Unlimited liability. Lacks status. Difficult to value, transfer and sell the business.

Partnership	Retain benefits of being self-employed. Share management and risk with other people. Has status, especially professional partnerships. Retirement plan can often be linked to the introduction of a new partner. Financial information not published.	Unlimited liability. Costs of drawing up a partnership agreement. Joint and several liability for the acts and roles (financial) of the other partners. Often difficult to value a partnership share.
Limited company	Liability limited to what you agreed to put in (via share purchase). Has status, especially a 'Plc'. Shares often easier to value, therefore more transferable and saleable.	Cost of forming a limited company. Annual audit cost(*) and return to Registrar of Companies. Memorandum and Articles of Association can limit directors' powers (although they can be changed). Financial information published at Companies House (abridged for small companies). * audit only required for companies with high turnover – £350,000 at time of writing.

Tax positions and remuneration

The two types of basic structure – Limited or Unlimited (including sole traderships, sole practitioners, and partnerships) – have different ways in which the owners can take their 'earnings' from the business, with different tax effects. It is important to understand the choices, and resulting limitations, available.

Unlimited

The owners earn the profits, and pay tax on them based on the year in which they are earned. They pay National Insurance based on the profits, within certain limits.

Limited

There are two principal groups involved here, the shareholders and the directors. In small and family companies they are often the same people. But their share of earnings is legally split between the two roles. Shareholders take their money in the form of dividends, which are not subject to National Insurance. Directors are employees and are paid a salary, which is subject to the rules of PAYE like any other salary.

Points to consider

Take a business that has generated £50,000 profit in the year, all of which is available to the 'owner' (whatever hat from the above list we deem him or her to be wearing). If the business is unlimited then a large portion of that will fall to higher rate taxation (40 per cent at the time of writing), which may not be 'cost-effective'. This would be particularly true if next year the business were to make no profit at all; in that year allowances and lower rate bands of tax would have been wasted although higher rate was paid the year previously.

But if that business were a limited company then it would pay only 21 per cent corporation tax (at the time of writing) although at that stage the money would still belong to the company and would not have yet come to the 'owners'. But if it could be so arranged then the owners might take out £25,000 in the first year and £25,000 in the second year, maximizing the use of allowances and bands and minimizing or eliminating tax at higher rates. Only a limited company can achieve this in that way, and is therefore useful where fluctuating profits are likely.

The limited company can also choose to distribute the year's amount in a mixture of salary and dividend. The salary element is, however, not only subject to PAYE deductions of tax and National Insurance but the company must pay to the government a sum for 'employers National Insurance' – effectively a tax which penalizes employment. The dividend does not attract any National Insurance, which can therefore be very 'cost effective'. However, one important point to note is that while all of profits count as 'earnings', only salary does, and not dividends. This means that a mortgage based on earnings cannot count the dividend element in its calculation. There are ways round such a situation with some mortgage brokers, such as 'self certifying' applications where proof of ability to pay only is required. But contributions to pension schemes can only be based on earnings, and this may be a deciding factor in planning taking money out of a limited company.

These, and many more complex situations involving tax planning, are one of the very purposes of engaging accountants; discuss the position with them to suit your trading and personal needs and to ensure that you do not fall foul of the law.

6 Franchising

FRANCHISING IS A very general term used to describe many different business arrangements whereby one party (the franchisor) agrees to sell to another party (the franchisee) the right to sell, use, distribute, develop, or market the franchisor's products, services, business systems, distribution chain, trademarks, etc.

In most franchising agreements the franchisee pays an initial sum to the franchisor, and then makes regular payments for an agreed period of time, dependent upon profits and/or turnover.

If you have an invention, a good idea, a business system or a formula that is successful there is nothing to stop you franchising it to a third party. Franchising recognizes that a company or an individual may not have the time and/or the capital to fully exploit a winning business formula, so the granting of the legal permission or licence to someone else to own and run a similar business helps exploit the success to gain market share before the competition can get organized.

Franchising is not a new concept: one of the earliest recorded examples in history was that of the Roman emperors granting tax collection powers to individuals for an 'up-front' lump sum. Nearer to home, most of us will have had a drink in a public house run by a tenant, the tenancy being a form of franchise.

To the question 'What can be franchised?', the answer is almost anything, so long as the two parties to the agreement can see the commercial gain. Franchising is considered to be an attractive route for people with capital or the ability to raise it, to purchase the right to own and run a tried and tested business formula, although the franchisor will impose certain trading conditions upon the franchisee which we shall consider later. Research has shown that while some 90 per cent of all new businesses fail within a five-year period, only 10 per cent of franchises meet a similar fate. Franchising is an increasingly popular way of starting a business, but one that can also result in costly mistakes.

On a visit to Singapore in the mid 1980s one of the authors was told the story of the McDonald's franchise in that country. Apparently the McDonald Corporation was looking for a suitable franchisee, and was having some difficulty in finding one as the perceived local wisdom was that it would be very difficult to sell Western fast food to a people who invented fast food and traditionally eat in fast food centres known as Hawker Centres. However, one enterprising Singaporean managed to negotiate a sole franchise for a period of time and became a multi-millionaire within two years.

We have already said that any sensible business system, product or service based, can be franchised, and the law of the market dictates how much you will pay for the franchise agreement, which in turn is based on the previous success of the franchisor. At the time of writing the capital investment necessary to purchase a franchise ranges between £3000 to £250,000. One of the most expensive is the Holiday Inn Corporation. If you feel that running a hotel is your dream the cost will be high, but the rewards also possibly so. One of the least expensive franchises, at £3400 plus VAT, is Cellars Ltd, if you wish to try your hand at the wine trade. A franchise from Kall Kwik, a well-known High Street name in printing, will set you back £40,000. Perfect Pizza can be yours for £35,000 and they already have 200 outlets and are proposing to open 80 new outlets over the next five years (from the time of writing). For the animal lover you can own a pet food delivery service for £8000 from Trophy Pet Foods, or the early bird can get a Unigate milkman franchise. Car lovers may be attracted to the shine of Autoglym car valeting products, while redundant spies, for £4950 plus VAT, may be seduced by Quantum, who franchise security equipment.

The opportunities would seem to be endless and more details can be obtained from the British Franchise Association – details at the end of the book. Further information about prospective franchises can be read in the national newspapers. Franchising fairs are held regularly in the major cities of the UK.

What type of business to choose

Choosing what type of business to buy is probably the most difficult decision the prospective franchisee has to make. From talking to franchisees a pattern is apparent, and for convenience we have listed them in three main groups.

Group one are the dreamers. They have probably been made redundant in their late forties to early fifties, have worked most of their lives in one industry and have received a lump sum and possibly a paid-up pension on termination of their employment. With their partner they have often talked and dreamed about running their own restaurant, pub or retail outlet. They normally have no expertise in these areas, and do not understand the skills and complexities needed to run a small business. Theirs is the highest failure rate; High Streets are full of closing down or closed restaurants, pubs and shops.

The second group we shall call 'more of the same'. These people have been in a particular trade most of their working lives and consider themselves to be experts. They bring to a new business their basic trade but forget that running a small business needs other skills such as customer and selling skills, keeping books of account, stock control and financial planning and control.

The third group we can call opportunistic. They investigate the market, analyse what skills they have got and realize that there are new ones to learn. They recognize that running a business should be judged by very cold criteria, such as 'Will the new business make money right away, i.e. have positive cashflow; can the business grow in the location chosen; are the products or services of high quality and good reputation and need only minimum stock holdings; and will the profits be enough to build up capital for the future?' The opportunistics are not so much influenced by what the business is, but more by what they can gain by running it.

Some people do, however, have the ability to learn a trade and then successfully become a franchisee.

Jim and Breda Fortune were the tenants of The Dartmouth Arms in Kentish Town. Jim came over to the UK from Ireland, and as a young man started working behind the bar. He learned the trade from cellar management, purchasing stock, keeping the books, engaging staff and customer skills. With Breda they eventually migrated to owning their own tenancy. Jim and Breda are a success story, and Jim's peculiar customer skills are legend throughout North London. However, statistics in the pub trade show that many retired policemen and sportsmen often take a pub and then fail. Why? Jim Fortune will tell you, 'You do not learn the pub trade from the customer side of the bar.' When questioned about how to run a pub, the Fortunes' philosophy is refreshingly simple: hard work, long hours, few holidays, keeping on top of the paperwork, retaining enough funds for quiet periods, having a sense of humour and above all putting quality and the customer first. Sound advice for all franchisees whatever the business.

Obviously in choosing what type of business to be in, common sense is your best ally. When considering the franchise of a meat boning business, 'vegetarians need not apply': desktop publishing and printing franchises are best suited to creative people; and people who are scared by heights do not make good roofers.

Financing the franchise

Most people who enter into franchising agreements have some capital to begin with, and/or they raise capital by sale of assets, investments or re-mortgaging their house. Financing a franchise is fundamentally no different to financing the purchase or start-up of any business. The initial investment in the franchise will usually cover how to run and operate your business, with specific details of how to source raw materials if any, up-front training, procedure manuals, quality requirements, initial advertising and promotional material, and help line etc. On top of this investment you will need sufficient capital for, say, premises, machinery and equipment, as well as working capital for stocks, office, factory or shop expenses, salaries and wages, and financing debtors if you need to grant credit to your customers. All these need to be evaluated and accounted for in your business plan, recommended for all potential franchisees, essential if you wish to borrow money from banks or other lenders. The amount of capital you will require will of course vary with the type of business you are considering. Kitting out a fast food outlet is going to be very much more expensive than the equipment needed to clean 'wheelie bins'. All the major High Street banks have specialist franchise sections who offer financial advice and assistance. The larger franchisors also give similar help and advice often at preferential rates, after all it is in their interest. Purchasing a franchise is of course risky, and for this reason we strongly recommend that you take professional advice from your solicitor, accountant and banker as well as the franchisor right at the outset.

The franchise agreement

The two parties to a franchise agreement can be likened to a partnership or a joint venture, and both parties will want it to succeed. But it is essential to take legal advice so as to establish exactly what you are buying, and what are the obligations of both parties. As we have said, what you are paying for is the right and know-how of how to run the franchise business as developed by the franchisor. This will include the 'how to do it' manual, training, marketing and sales prospects and promotions and in some cases specialist tools and equipment and initial stock to get you started. The franchising agreement will also address the following issues:

- The cost of the initial up-front investment payable to the franchisor.
- The fees you will pay monthly, quarterly or whatever to the franchisor for the right to continue to work the business.
- The initial help and assistance you will be given, e.g. training, marketing advice, help to locate suitable offices or retail premises, etc.
- The after-sales service, if any, e.g. the services of a trouble-shooter.
- The territorial area you can operate within.
- The amount if any you will be required to contribute to advertising and promotion of the products/services as created and developed by the franchisor, usually a percentage of your gross turnover.
- The parts of the business system that the franchisor is responsible for, and normally functions of the franchisor's head office, e.g. monitoring the quality of products/services throughout all the franchisee units, new product/service development, promotion and advertising, central buying function, debt collection, etc.

- The parts of the business system that you the franchisee will be responsible for, such as maintaining the quality or the product/service, fair employment practices, keeping proper books of account so that the franchisor can collect what is due, and levels of performance.
- Reasons why and how the agreement can be terminated.
- Provision for eventualities such as the death of the franchisee and how the business may be sold or otherwise disposed of.

The above list is neither exhaustive or exclusive, and each franchising contract will need careful reading and explanation.

Investigating the franchisor

Before signing the franchise agreement you will wish to gather as much information as possible about the franchisor. We recommend the following course of action:

- As most franchisors are limited companies you can obtain copies of past and current reports and accounts from Companies House. These you can discuss with your accountant if you are not used to reading balance sheets. Alternatively ask your accountant or solicitor to do the investigation for you.
- Ask your bank to obtain a banker's reference for you.
- Visit at least two of the franchisor's outlets, and if possible talk to the franchisees about their business. Try the products and/or services. Most importantly take a friend along with you; you may not be as objective as you should be at this stage of the investigation.
- Try 'mystery shopping'. Visit the franchise as a customer and put your enquiries to the test not as a direct question but just by using the franchise as any member of the public would. Does it seem to come up to what you want? Can you see a way to make your franchise of that business work better still?
- Visit the franchisor's Head Office and discuss their business plans. Seek detailed information about the costs of running the business, gross and net margins and any other pertinent business and financial information.
- If available, read all the promotional and advertising material including the franchisor's newsletter.

- If practicable, work in one of the franchisor's outlets, to get hands-on experience and the feel of the business.
- If you have access to the Internet ask questions about the franchisor. What you are looking for is adverse press comments, which may impact upon the reputation of the business.

The advantages of franchising

Some of the advantages of franchising have already been mentioned in this chapter, other main advantages are as follows:

- Many franchises are household names, with an enviable reputation in the market place, e.g. Body Shop.
- As a franchisee you are the owner of the business, you take the risks, but you are entitled to all the rewards.
- You will have the backing of the franchisor who can offer guidance, advice and support at every level of the business.
- You will be trained to run the business and given a procedure manual of how to operate day to day.
- You will benefit from the economies of scale, such as discounts from preferred suppliers, bulk discounts for stock, and national advertising and promotional campaigns.
- You will have your own territory to operate in.
- You will be given market information as collected by the Head Office, and will be entitled to market new product/service developments.
- Some franchisors offer preferential finance rates for new franchisees.
- The major banks understand franchising and support the concept, which is a great help when negotiating working capital requirements.
- You will be building a business that should generate sound profits as well as capital growth.
- The risk on entry is less than starting a totally new business.

The disadvantages of franchising

Again some of the disadvantages have already been listed previously. Other disadvantages that need to be considered are as follows:

- Although you own your own business, you will still have to operate it within the controls set by the franchisor and written into the agreement. These controls are normally associated with procedures, performance and quality standards.
- Some people become too dependent upon the franchisor, which can kill initiative, drive and entrepreneurial flair.
- Business mistakes by either other franchisees or the franchisors can lead to bad publicity which may cascade down to all the outlets.
- The franchisor may initiate commercial mistakes leading to unsaleable products/services.
- The level of support and quality coming from the Head Office may change for the worse. One major franchise for whom we were able to examine the records of over two dozen outlets were finding very high turnover rates of franchisees because the Head Office was perceived as failing to promote the product but instead was using unethical tricks to lock franchisees into financial handcuffs.
- As a franchisee you will be locked in to suppliers, and other business arrangements where if totally independent you could purchase these goods/services cheaper.
- In organizations where there are franchisees and company-owned outlets, preference and advantages may be given to the self-owned units.
- There will be restrictions on how you may sell or otherwise dispose of your business.

Conclusion

Franchising would appear to be one of the more successful routes for people to run their own business. With sufficient capital to invest you can acquire the right to operate a tried and tested profitable business formula in your own territory. The risks are less than setting up your own business from scratch, and the figures show that nearly 90 per cent of all franchisees are still trading after the five-year watershed. Franchising is not a soft option – most franchisees work extremely hard and often very long hours, but they are prepared to pay that price for independence. Some franchisees acquire more than one franchise within the same organization, and create their own business empire.

If after reading this chapter you are considering franchising then we strongly recommend that you get in contact with the British Franchise Association whose address is given at the end of this book.

They are the experts at franchising and can advise at all levels of the franchising operation. We also recommend that you attend one of the franchising fairs which are advertised in the national and local press where you will be able to see and speak to many franchisors.

7 / The New Construction Industry Scheme

EFFECTIVE FROM 1 August 1999 the Inland Revenue, as part of its major overhaul of tax administration, has changed the rules and regulations relating to those self-employed people working within the construction industry. The changes were much heralded with outline information in the Finance Acts 1995 and 1996 but the final regulations were only set down on 23 October 1998.

Every subcontractor has to register with the Inland Revenue to obtain either a Gross Payment Certificate or a Registration Card. If neither are obtained then the subcontractor cannot be paid by a main contractor for work done. No other industry or trade requires registration of this nature with the Inland Revenue; the goal must presumably be to try to limit the number of people working in the so-called 'black economy', i.e. evading paying their taxes, which is still believed to be rife within the construction industry.

The Inland Revenue informed us, on enquiry, that pressure for these changes had been from within the construction industry itself, an approach initiated by the largest firms in the industry.

If you are a subcontractor

You will have to apply for either a Gross Payment Certificate (GPC), or a Registration Card. To qualify for a GPC you will have to demonstrate that:

• You are in the construction industry providing labour to carry on construction work.

- Your business is conducted mostly through a bank account.
- You maintain proper books and records in accordance with the Taxes Act.
- You send in appropriate returns to the Inland Revenue relating to the construction industry scheme.
- You run the business from 'proper' premises with 'proper' equipment, stock and facilities.
- You meet the turnover test.

The Inland Revenue do not define their term 'proper' but the intention seems to have been to try to discourage those working from home. Since the system relates only to the supply of labour and not to materials and equipment it is hard to see why such businesses could not be run from home, and indeed many are. It is possible that the phrasing is simply one of many such terms applied by tax law to provide a 'catch-all' excuse for refusal if one is needed. There is, as yet, no formal statement that those working from home will be refused.

The turnover test was introduced 'softly'. The initial information – for example *CIS FACT 1* issued in 1997 – suggested the turnover requirement was likely to be £20,000 to £30,000 per annum. In fact on introduction the following year it was set at a base of £30,000. It was informally suggested by one Inland Revenue officer we spoke to that there was a belief that subcontractors failed to declare all their income, and that some would adjust their declarations – and pay nearer to the appropriate tax – by only as much as they thought might be needed to qualify. By implying the limit would be low, many would then fail to qualify for GPCs which was what the Inland Revenue wanted all along. They have always tried to contain subcontractors within either the PAYE scheme or the 'old' SC60 scheme which deducted tax at source (as the Registration Card system will do).

The turnover requirement

The turnover requirement is £30,000 per annum for an individual or £200,000 per annum for partnerships or companies. Partnerships may also apply a multiple of individual partners' thresholds. As indicated in the 23 October 1998 press release, 'turnover' includes 'income, net of the cost of materials, received for construction work, whether carried out within or outside the [Construction Industry] Scheme.' This means that if a proportion of the income is earned on domestic or private work where the Scheme does not apply it can nonetheless count as part of the total.

To check if your turnover qualifies take a three-year period, during which the turnover for at least two of the years exceeds the threshold and the average turnover over all three years meets 90 per cent of the average of the thresholds for those years, or a period of six or fewer consecutive tax months in which the turnover is at least 70 per cent of the annual threshold (i.e. 70 per cent of £30,000 = £21,000). The three years can be any three without reference to accounting reference periods but must all be contained within four years prior to the date of application.

Smaller partnerships do not have to meet the £200,000 limit. They may also apply on the basis of the individual number of partners times the threshold limit, i.e. a three partner partnership would have to exceed three times £30,000 i.e. £90,000. The rules for years to be considered are the same as for individuals.

The £200,000 threshold, if used, is also examined over a three-year period on the same basis as above.

Companies have the same choices. They have the £200,000 threshold or an alternative based on the number of directors. In the case of 'closely controlled companies', i.e. usually 'family' companies, the shareholders are used in the calculation. Therefore such a company with two directors and three shareholders (two of whom are the directors) the turnover threshold would be £90,000 (three times £30,000).

There are more complex calculations based on the same base figures for more complex corporate structures, for example, partnerships which have companies as one or more of the partners. These cases are outside the scope of this book, and such companies should discuss their situation with their advisors or directly with the Inland Revenue.

If you are a contractor

Each contractor, i.e. individual, partnership or company, who engages subcontractors must take the following steps to ensure they comply with the new regulations:

- First, to decide if the contract in question falls within the scheme. This includes permanent or temporary building works involving site preparation, construction, alteration, painting and decorating, repairs, or demolition.
- Second, to examine the working relationship with the subcontractor to determine if the nature of the engagement falls within the scope of PAYE, i.e. should the subcontractor be regarded as employed or self-employed in this relationship.
- Third, assuming that the relationship is one of self-employed subcontractor to inspect the card presented. This can be either a Registration Card or a Gross Payment Certificate. Such certificates or cards need only be examined once during the period of the contract providing the certificate or card is valid throughout. If the contract extends beyond the expiry date of the certificate or card then the replacement must be examined after that expiry date before further payments are made. Those holding GPCs can be paid in full. Those holding only Registration Cards can be paid only with a deduction of tax which itself is then paid over to the Revenue.
- Each month the appropriate vouchers must be submitted for the payments made, within fourteen days of the end of the month. These are Gross Payment Vouchers for payments to those holding GPCs; Company Gross Payment Vouchers for payments to companies holding Company GPCs; or Taxed Payment Vouchers for payments to those for whom tax was deducted before payment was made.
- Any deducted tax under the Scheme must be paid over to the Inland Revenue. This can be done with any PAYE deducted tax and National Insurance if appropriate. This must be done within fourteen days of the end of the month.
- Each year an annual return of all payments is to be made.

8 Business Plans

Most businesses at some time have – at start-up or later – to borrow money or arrange overdrafts. Some need to encourage investment from others on a large scale in order to grow. This requires the skill of 'selling' your business to financiers, bankers, and others. The principles of this selling are the same as for any other selling: speak the language of the buyer, think in terms of what the reader of the plans expects to see. Be sure that you have presented your best picture of your business, but in a way that will answer the questions of that reader who is going to make the decision to lend to you, or to otherwise financially invest in your company.

However, the business plan is not just for others. It is one of the most important documents that you can prepare for yourself. At the outset it is your way of committing your aspirations to paper to first sell the business to the most important 'buyer' of all – YOU. It is very easy to lie back and dream of your business, and of your successes. People, they say, are either inherently optimistic or pessimistic; the optimist will dwell on the good points, on the anticipated successes and may go ahead with a faulty business idea because he or she has not thought through the problems that will emerge. The pessimist on the other hand will focus on the fears and the possible problems and will not make a move, unaware of the compensating advantages and strengths. By committing the whole business plan to paper, with a view to convincing yourself of its strengths and weaknesses as if you were a third party, you have the best possible chance of highlighting the correct balance of good and bad to come. Even good ideas do not convert into feasible business plans without research, thought and effort. Far too many business plans are amateurish, naive, not thought through and with an unacceptable risk factor for both the bank and you.

Many people starting their own business get carried away with the non-urgent and non-essential items of business life. People spend far too much time, effort and money initially on such items as prestige offices, factory space and machinery, office machines, furniture, carpets, letterheads, business cards, advertising and promotional material, and forget if not neglect that for survival and success sales are the most important issue. The business plan lets you see the areas where you most need to target resource.

The business plan can be divided into two main sections: the financial and the non-financial. Many businesses that start up do so without any business plan at all, which is not sensible, but the majority of those that do have a plan usually have only the financial aspects: cashflow, profit predictions, perhaps costings, and so on. Very few business plans compiled by small businesses think of the non-financial components unless specifically asked for by, say, a bank manager.

The financial component

At its simplest level the business plan is a prediction of the income and expenditure that you believe you will achieve once the business has started, or after you have implemented a proposed change to the business, or undertaken an expansion or contraction in activities.

It is first 'presented' to yourself, and later it will probably be presented to your bankers or other sources of funds. It may be presented to your accountant (who will hopefully have worked with you on its preparation) so that he or she can use it to promote your business to raise funds or investment.

It should be a realistic plan, but that is not to say that you are not entitled to be optimistic as well. You will need the energy of optimism to run a business, and it would be tragic to lose it at this early stage. However, such optimism must not be allowed to cloud your view of the reality. So, for example, you may be entitled to project your forthcoming earnings on the basis of contracts likely though not yet firmly tied up. But at the same time you should have some awareness of the consequences of not gaining that contract. The plan can have a 'lowest' and 'highest' range and should set out your assumptions so that others can read it clearly.

But it is not your job to paint the dark side of the picture; bank managers and others are perfectly capable of being gloomy without your help. It is one of those rather bizarre games of negotiating that they will expect you to present a rose-tinted picture and they will mentally 'tone it down', so you have to be fairly rose-tinted so as not to be *too* toned down.

The business plan should set out your reasoning and any background information that you have used to arrive at your predictions (such as numbers of clients, diversity of clients, fees likely to be receivable, costs to be incurred, capital expenditures, etc.).

Such detail allows for others – and you – to challenge your assumptions. If you do not, life eventually will and possibly at far greater cost.

The financial information you should ensure you have to hand, and have good knowledge of, must include:

- An analysis of the set-up costs, specifying (by month) when you will have to make outlays. There are often very heavy 'up-front' investments to be made in assets and staffing; is the finance in place, and will it be sustained by, say, the bank long enough for you to start recovering the costs through sales or income?
- Capital outlays (what large, expensive items will need purchasing/leasing and how long they will last before needing replacement). Have you considered whether to buy them, or lease them? Can you share certain such assets with others at least in the short term?
- An analysis of the day-to-day running costs, specifying when you will have to make outlays. Day to day you will have to find regular chunks of money; make sure you know how much and when. For the business to last even into the medium term you must be sure that eventually the day-to-day income will outweigh the costs. Time to quote the oft-quoted Mr Micawber from *David Copperfield*: 'Annual income twenty pounds, annual expenditure nineteen nineteen six, result happiness. Annual income twenty pounds, annual expenditure twenty pounds ought and six, result misery.'

- The financial safety-net/contingency fund to hand (have you got any reserves personally in case all does not go as predicted?). If not, then what would be the consequences: could you lose your home? Have you discussed that risk with your relationship-partner? Are you perhaps relying on their income from employment to sustain you through the start-up period and if so how do they feel about that?
- The financial safety-net/contingency fund needed. Never mind what you have or haven't got – have you considered what you might reasonably need! If you have a reasonable chance of needing to draw from personal reserves and they are simply not there then your whole business idea might be just too risky. Think. And discuss with your family – they will be affected in some way for certain.
- Projected Profit and Loss Statement (how much money are you going to make – and when). Having worked out the monies you are going to make and the monies you are going to spend, and on what, you are in a position to put the whole lot together into a summary known as the Profit and Loss Account, a projected version of the accounts you will eventually historically produce for the taxman and others. This is the document that tells you a lot about the medium term. Is it profit or loss? If it is profit, is it enough to keep your investment alive in the business? If profit, is it enough or would you be better just getting a job? If a loss, how long will that loss be before it turns into a profit and can you sustain the business for that period of time? If a loss, what can you do to lessen the loss, what costs can be cut or controlled, or dealt with another way? What additional income might realistically be possible?
- Projected Balance Sheet. A summary of the assets and liabilities that you will own and owe at the end of your first year. What capital assets? What money in the bank? What money owed to you by others? What do you owe others? What overdraft? How much will you have invested in the business? If you owe more than you own how long can you sustain that position?
- Projected Cashflow Statement (when you are going to get money in and pay money out – quite different to the Profit and Loss Statement). See the next section below.
- Your projected drawings from the business (how much do you need to take out to live on?). The self-employed often have an unfortunate tendency not to take out a proper salary for

themselves. They undervalue themselves, or fail to meet the needs of their lifestyles and their families' needs. You are a cost that must be met; remember to treat yourself as such.

- Loans, overdrafts and other facilities required. Also, what security – if any – you are prepared to offer, e.g. a charge over the assets of the business or over personal assets such as your house.
- Any grants to be applied for, as well as capital to be introduced by the owner(s) and capital from any other sources.
- If you are taking over an existing business, a brief history together with historical financial information including cashflows, profit and loss accounts, balance sheets and current financial arrangements.

Cashflow forecast

The cashflow forecast is a part of budgeting; it predicts inflows and outflows of cash for a period ahead. A typical layout for a cashflow forecast would be as in Figure 8.1.

In Figure 8.1 you can compare the first three months' actual cashflows with anticipated cashflows. You will not be so concerned where your predictions were fairly accurate; for example, predicted cash sales for February were within a reasonable range of the actual results. In addition there are certain predictions which you know will be accurate from the outset, for example rent and rates are usually predetermined months and, in the case of rent, often years ahead. However, you should look at those areas where there is considerable diversity from your anticipated figures. This is known as exception reporting, i.e. devoting your attention to those areas where there is the greatest difference from what you expected.

For example, cash sales in March were £1200 whereas you had only expected them to be £600. There may be several factors involved and your understanding of them will enable you to better anticipate the year ahead:

- You may have commissioned a large marketing campaign in the first months of the year, which was not anticipated when drawing up the forecast at the end of the previous year, but which has resulted in increased sales.
- There may be some factor in the market which has accelerated the sales you would have had over, say, the first nine months

of the year into the first three months, and particularly into March. Identifying that will enable you to recognize that far from being a pattern of increase there will be reduced cash sales in future months.

- Your services may be in much greater demand than anticipated and if you can identify that then you might predict considerably increased cash sales in the months ahead.
- You may have made cash sales at the expense of credit sales and, if so, then you should be anticipating reduced income from debtors in the next quarter.
- It appears that your credit sales in January 1999 (received in March 1999) were higher than anticipated: £4800 as opposed to £2700. This may be the case and examination of the sales patterns will confirm this.
- However, it may be that you had anticipated your clients paying on the usual terms, but they paid early, in which case you cannot now expect their payments in future months; your anticipation of future months should be reduced.
- On the other hand you may have made more sales resulting in the increased income and you might identify that the trend will continue; you can anticipate increased funds in the months ahead.

When you look at the pattern of purchases (higher increases than anticipated towards the later months) you can begin to see that you probably *have* made more sales, requiring the purchase of more goods for sale. On the other hand the increased pattern of purchases may reflect an inappropriate optimism for the months ahead. You should ensure that the purchase requirements are being based on a proper understanding of the sales and debt collection patterns and not on a misunderstanding which results in overstocking and over-optimism.

You also have a £2000 bill falling due in February 1999 which was not anticipated. Naturally you will want to know why that has arisen. You might also want to know why this had not been anticipated since in reality you should have had some forewarning of this expenditure; not having processed that into the forecast suggests something at fault.

In particular you can see that the company's closing bank balance is not as anticipated. By the end of the first quarter it has a closing bank balance of £4915 whereas you had anticipated a

CASHFLOW FORECAST CHART 1999	Forecast Jan.	Actual Jan.	Forecast Feb.	Actual Feb.	Forecast March	Actual March	Forecast April	Actual April	Forecast May	Actual May	Forecast June	Actual June
Opening Bank Balance b/fwd	2000	2000	6250	6490	7680	5790	5480		5810		8770	
Income												
from Sales (Cash)	1000	1300	200	170	600	1200	400		600		200	
from Sales (Debtors)	5000	5000	2600	2800	2700	4800	1800		3900		3300	
from Interest earned					30	35						40
from VAT recoverable												
from Other Sources (Sundry)							20					
Income Subtotal	6000	6300	2800	2970	3330	6035	2220		4500		3540	
Expenditure												
for Purchases (Cash)	200	240	200	240	50	460	200		50		600	
for Purchases (on Credit)	800	800	600	650	500	700	900		800		700	

Salaries and Wages (Net)	300	300	200	200	200	250	200	200	200
PAYE Payments	70	70	70	70	70	70	70	70	70
Rent/Rates					1500	1500			1000
Light/Heat/ Telephone	330	350			100	80	400		100
Interest Charges									
HP Payments	50	50	50	50	50	50	50	50	50
VAT Payments			200	210				300	
Advertising Promotions			50	250	60	800	70	70	70
Capital Expenditure									
Other (Specify)									
Legal Fees				2000					
Dividend Payments					3000	3000			6000
Expenditure Subtotal	1750	1810	1370	3670	5530	6910	1890	1540	8720
Closing Bank Balance c/fwd	6250	6490	7680	5790	5480	4915	5810	8770	3590

Figure 8.1 A typical cashflow forecast

closing bank balance of £5480. The advantage given by the increase in sales has been more than wiped out by the large unexpected cost. This may mean that the company will go into overdraft at some time later, or earlier than anticipated in the cashflow forecast chart, and you should contact the bank and arrange the necessary anticipated finances based on your new information.

Given a different set of data you might have found that you were going to be unexpectedly cash rich and rather than waiting until a later date to put funds on high-interest earnings deposit you might transfer some sooner.

It is at this now fairly advanced stage in the cashflow budgeting cycle where many business people fail to make the next and most important step. The cashflow forecast should not be regarded as static. All too often having gone through the 'cashflow process' people then allow their 'actual' columns to fill up throughout the year and steadily watch an increase in diversity between the prediction and the actual. The important point about cashflow forecasting is that it is a continuous cycle, requiring constant maintenance and update.

Having processed the result of the first three months you should then use the information gleaned from your analysis of the differences between prediction and actual to completely rewrite the next twelve months ahead.

You could budget for profit and loss in the same way as you have budgeted for cashflow. The template for the year ahead would superficially look very similar. There would, however, be a number of significant differences, a mention of which enables comparison and contrasting of the cash flow with the profit and loss statements:

- There would be a difference of timing. For example, sales are reported in the profit and loss account in the months of the sale whereas the cash inflow may be months later. Similarly with purchases, and indeed any bills paid on credit terms.
- Income and expenditures are shown net of VAT in the profit and loss forecast (as the net VAT from sales and purchases is paid over to the government and does not belong to the company), whereas the figures in the cashflow forecast are shown gross, i.e. including VAT, since that is the amount that will actually come into or go out of your bank.

- The profit and loss account will 'spread' overheads whereas the cashflow forecast predicts actual payment dates. If, for example, we take the light, heat and telephone anticipated costs for the year the cashflow forecast predicts them as £330 in January 1999, £400 in April 1999, (and, say, £150 in July 1999 and £200 in October 1999) as this reflects the dates when these bills will actually be paid. However, the total anticipated bills for the year of £1080 would probably be spread evenly throughout the year in a profit and loss forecast, i.e. £90 per month (possibly adjusted for known seasonal fluctuations but still not adjusted so far as to reflect actual bill payment dates).
- Hire purchase payments will be separated with the profit and loss account bearing the monthly interest charge whereas in the cashflow forecast the total amount payable will be shown.
- Capital expenditure will not appear in the profit and loss forecast as capital expenditures are not applicable to profit and loss.
- Proprietor's drawings will not appear in the profit and loss forecast as, again, these are not part of those expenditures.
- The opening and closing bank balances will not be shown on the profit and loss forecast as these are not applicable to that document.
- Depreciation, which is not a flow of actual cash, is an overhead and will be shown on the profit and loss account figures.

The non-financial component

The Business Plan is not just a financial statement. It should also contain the following written sections:

- *Your training/qualifications/experience.* Give a brief history (CV) of the owner(s) highlighting experience and business success. Similarly the training, qualifications and experience of other partners or key people in your proposed business structure. Why do you think you can succeed in this business? Do you have a background in that sector of industry, commerce or retail? Is it a business where your clients might expect you to have qualifications (e.g. accountant), and do you have the appropriate ones? If there are other people involved do they offer the same, or indeed do they fill in the gaps in your own qualities? Analysis of who is going to be involved often uncovers harsh but necessary realities: are you employing Uncle Bill because he's qualified or for some sympathetic family reason? The latter reason could cost you dearly in many ways. The written analysis of you and those around you forces you to think through your business-mindedness.

- *A description of the business/service you are offering.* If you are selling, will it be through a shop, or a mobile van, or through mail order? If a service, do you offer home visits? Do you have an office clients can visit or will you work from home? If the latter, are clients and customers welcome? And how will your customers view the way you have decided to answer these questions? How do your answers stack up against your opposition?

- *Your unique selling point* (USP), i.e. your main advantages over existing or similar products/services.

- *Customer profile/target market* (i.e. who do you think you will get as clients and why do you think you can get them?). Is there likely to be an untapped market and if so why do you think you can reach them when your competitors have failed? If there is not an untapped market then you will have to take your market share from your competitors; why do you think you can? What is it that you are offering them that will make your potential customers or clients move from their present suppliers?

- *A detailed analysis of the market,* such as age group, socio-economic group, geographical locations and where they presently go for the product/service.

- *Proposed catchment area for clients* (how many clients are there in the geographical area you are proposing to operate in?). Is the number sufficient to sustain your business? How many of them can you reasonably expect to attract? How long will it take you to attract sufficient numbers before the business starts 'paying its way'?

- *Your proposed prices, fees, charges.* Did you arrive at the price by costing, knowing that the price will cover your costs and provide you with profit, or did you just take the prevailing market price which you might find is insufficient to sustain the business as you set it up? If the price you will have to charge, because it is what the market will stand, cannot sustain your business then what can you do to change your costs so that it *will* sustain your business? If you cannot bring the two together then your business is not viable.

- *Comparison with competitors' charges.* If you are proposing to charge more than your competitors why do you think they will pay – what else/extra are you offering?
- *Analysis of the competition.* How well organized are they? Do they offer all of the services you are proposing (visit to clients' homes for example)? If they do not offer what you are proposing to offer is it because you believe they overlooked it (unlikely), could not organize it (possible), or because they have already found it uneconomical and not worth doing (quite possible)?
- *Results of market research.* Is the market growing or contracting? Are prices likely to rise in the future, or fall? Are there new technologies around the corner that will make your product or service gradually – or rapidly! – obsolete?
- *Proposed premises* (type, location, costs). Will you work from home or from business premises? How accessible will your premises be for your clients? Do they need to visit? Will they be put off if they find getting to you inconvenient?
- For a manufacturing set-up, a simple diagram or flow chart showing the stages from sourcing of raw materials to finished goods.
- For importers and retailers, a similar flow chart indicating sources of goods in partly or finished form and security of supply.
- *Time frame for start-up and development of the business.* What's the kick-off date? Are you ready? Is the financing in place? Are your staff in place and ready for 'the off'? Is your stationery ready? And a thousand other 'are you ready' questions to lie awake at night and ponder for a month . . .
- *A 'vision' of how your ideal business will look when fully up and running.* If you want a successful business then take a while to sit quietly in a room and imagine the best possible outcome you can reasonably expect, and truly want. See yourself in a large well-decorated office with six or seven staff. See yourself strolling through your hi-tech factory watching a thousand staff and robots producing your high-quality products. Or however you want to see yourself . . . Now write down your dreams. And now take a look at the plans you've made for the immediate future and ask if they reasonably lead to

your hoped for outcome. If not, and if your dreams are real ambitions, then re-plan and re-think. Once you're 'under way' you'll have less and less time to plan and think through the direction of the business: even the best entrepreneurs find themselves carried along by the current to some extent. This is your last chance to be sure you're doing what you *really* want to do.

When writing and presenting your business plan, it will be useful to bear in mind the following:

- Banks and other professional lenders have an understanding and detailed knowledge of most business ventures. They can tell the difference between sound commercial sense and uninformed hype.
- Keep the business plan as short as makes sense. Smaller, well thought out and well-constructed documents will have a higher impact than long-winded and padded tomes.
- Presentation is very important. The business plan should be professionally typed, bound and indexed and include any press and trade information concerning your product/service.

In our discussions with bank managers about the quality and impact and the most common flaws in business plans their comments were as follows:

- The majority of sales projections are seriously overstated, particularly in the first two years of trading, and this is the major contributor to business failure.
- Most business plans underestimate the initial capital including working capital (debtors, stock, cash less creditors and short-term loan repayments) needed to run the business for the first three years of trading, which is the most critical period. Do not ask for too little funding; better to over-borrow and repay surplus funds back to the lender rather than having to ask for more.

A friend of one of the authors was a career banker of the 'old school' where honesty, integrity and respect for the customer was just as important as business plans. He quotes the dictum that a good banker lends to people as well as projections.

Expansion

The business plan should be revised and updated regularly, even if there is no obvious perceived reason for it, because it serves as a focus to keep the owner aware of changes in his or her business that he or she might not be properly aware of. It may also help when considering major changes, such as finding new funding to expand or buy out a competitor.

There are important considerations to bring in here. If you want to raise funding for your company, i.e. get someone to inject cash into the business for you to use for re-equipping, or for expansion, and so on, then you have basically two choices. You can find people to buy shares in your company (if you are a limited company) or take a partnership arrangement with you and pay for their 'stake', providing the money. Or you can borrow money from banks or other lenders. What are the advantages and disadvantages of each course of action? What are the risks? How do you decide which course of action to take?

Shares/partnership

Advantages	*Disadvantages*
Other people share the risk with you.	If the business is successful other people now own part of it.
You may introduce new expertise with your new people.	The other people involved may wish to move the business in a direction that does not suit you.
If the venture is not as profitable as hoped the 'servicing' of the money need not be paid – i.e. no dividend or partnership share.	

Borrowing

Advantages	*Disadvantages*
If the business is successful then you end up with the whole business in your ownership.	If the business is not successful the servicing of the loan (interest) still has to be paid and can bankrupt the business.

9 / Work from Home or Not?

PROBABLY THE FIRST question that most self-employed people ask is whether or not to work from home or take business premises. For some businesses the decision is made by the nature of the business – a shop or factory for example. But for many the choice is open, and how do you decide? Set out below are the two basic ways in which you can follow a trade or profession, setting out the good and bad points to consider: working from home, or working from premises.

Working from home: Advantages

Costs
- *Keeps overheads (expenses) to a minimum.* You already pay the costs of running your home. This decision will avoid having to pay rent and business rates, additional insurance, telephone, gas and electricity bills and will probably avoid the purchase of office equipment and furniture, some of which you may have in your home, or at least which existing resources can be adapted to provide (working on the dining-room table instead of buying a desk, etc.).
- *No travelling costs.* Commuting from the bedroom to the dining room is the cheapest form of transport yet devised.
- *Added security over assets.* There is usually someone on the premises, you or your family, and this is obvious to would-be burglars. Offices are usually closed over weekends making them an easy target for break-ins. (That said, homes get burgled too and then you might lose personal and business items.)

Environment

You have control over the ambience and environment in which you will be working. This is particularly true if the choice is between this and visiting clients in their homes, but may also be true where costs may not allow you to design the office with the ambience you would prefer.

Personal

- *You have control over the times you do and don't work*, allowing you to be very flexible to your clients' needs, your own needs and those of your family. If you wake up in the middle of the night restless you always have the opportunity to go to your desk and get some work done (if it becomes a habit you're in trouble!). You can do routine work in front of the TV. When there is a rush job on that needs overtime to get it completed it is easy to arrange; you've never left the office after all.
- *Work can be arranged around domestic commitments*. For many people self-employment must fit in around domestic issues. Parents for example have school 'runs' to do at fixed times. Working from home, where clients expect to make appointments and not just 'call in unexpected' helps here. In addition, you don't have to permanently leave work at 3.30 p.m. when collecting the children from school; having got them back home you are free to continue working providing they are safe and occupied.
- *No travelling time*. A good many hours are spent by those in offices just getting there and back. That time can be spent directly working, or with family and friends.
- *No need to transport equipment*. For some people their work requires equipment. For example, reflexologists need a couch-bed on which to work and those who choose to visit clients in their own homes need to transport them with them. In addition, such 'part-time' practitioners might not permanently rent premises but if avoiding working from home they may hire premises a few days a week – that usually entails carrying the couch-beds from home and back every time they work. Working from home prevents that problem.
- *You will probably feel relaxed in your own surroundings*. (Though this will depend on the nature of your home; an office in a

house with very vocal toddlers might not leave you feeling relaxed when a major client telephones!)

Working from home: Disadvantages

Costs
- *You may become liable for business rates.* If in doubt you should contact your local authority before setting up.
- *You may become liable for Capital Gains Tax when selling the property later.* As your home your property is currently exempt from this tax, but if used for business some of the gain may become taxable.

Environment
- *It is easy to become distracted during work if domestic difficulties arise.* Young children at home, knowing one or both of their parents are also present, naturally expect attention unless (and sometimes even if) you have a nanny present (paid, grandmother, or whoever). And of course cuts and bruises that nanny can easily deal with demand a parent's attention in a child's eye if the parent is known to be there. Most parents would in any case find such a situation hard to ignore.
- *Sometimes the effect of working from home must be viewed from other peoples' points of view.* When our client Gerry Zierler of Zierler Media:Targeted Television moved from a home environment to an outside office due to substantial business expansion his son commented that 'at last I can bring my friends home again'.
- *You need to ensure that your home fulfils safety and hygiene requirements.* Business premises, particularly those where staff or visitors may be present, need certain standards not demanded in the home. And some businesses – say, cake or sandwich making for public consumption – demand certain standards of hygiene that may be difficult in a home with pets and lively children.
- *Working from home can be very isolating;* some people prefer to work with others around them to 'spark them off' creatively.
- *A professional atmosphere can be difficult to maintain in a home environment* without losing the ambience of the home, or creating stress and tension in other family members. To make an office look 'office-like' in a room in the house is relatively

easy but if you have to see clients how do you get them to that room without going through your family hallway, perhaps past the children's toys, and so on?

Personal

- *It can be difficult to forget work when your papers are near to hand.* Any break in the family activities can result in the self-employed person going to their desk, starting work, and being 'lost' to the family for the remainder of that day or evening.
- *You could create arguments with your neighbours* if, for example, your clients park over their drives, or make noise at unsociable hours.
- *You may breach local authority/lease/covenant restrictions on the use of your home.* You should check with the relevant authorities or documents, or seek the advice of the Citizens' Advice Bureau or a solicitor.
- Although your own home may seem like a place of security remember that during the day when most people are at work many homes are empty – there may be fewer people about in your road during the day than there would be in office environments.
- *Family pets can be both distracting to clients and unprofessional in the atmosphere they create.* Some businesses may be prevented from operating on those grounds alone; for example a food preparation business.
- You may have less control over unscheduled visitors such as family, salesmen, or telephone calls, and so on.

Working from a specified workplace: Advantages

Costs

None – it's costly! But the other advantages may make this desirable nonetheless.

Environment

- It is easier to create and maintain a professional image in an office environment.
- You may attract 'walk-in' trade off the street which is unlikely in a home environment and probably unsafe in many cases anyway.

- You can engage in higher-profile advertising such as a sign board. Your neighbours are unlikely to welcome your erecting a flashing neon sign in your front garden!
- Other businesses and existing clients may feel it is easier to recommend you to their valued colleagues if your image is more professional.

Personal
- There is no – or at least less – disruption to family life and intrusion into home environment.
- You have the ability to get away from work and spend quality time with your family, having left the job behind at the office.
- You may find working in groups, or with others similarly focused on work, inspiring and creative.

Working from a specified workplace: Disadvantages

Costs
- The outlay of setting up an office can be a drain on much needed resources right at the beginning when the uncertainties of success are most dangerously poised.
- The costs throughout the life of the business are higher: costs of lease or rent, or premises mortgage; costs of office utilities; business rates; and so on. This means the business must make more profits just to cover itself monthly. You must be sure that the office will pay its way by increasing your potential.
- There may be increased travelling costs to and from the office.

Environment
It may be more difficult to create and maintain your own environment and ambience the way you like it. You may be restricted by the terms of business leases, etc.

Personal
- You may be limited in the hours you can offer to clients if, for example, you work in serviced offices that shut down after a certain time, or on industrial estates that are uninviting late at night.

- There may be increased overall time spent 'at work' because of having to travel.

Other considerations

Consider that even though you might decide that the business will need to operate from premises at some time it may not be essential to do so from the beginning. You could set up from home, then move to offices or other premises at a later date. On the other hand, to some extent you will be defining your style of business and you may lose the clients and customers you need to attract by not projecting the right image from the start. You must consider how you would grow from home if necessary, and if you think it is too limiting to begin in that way then your business plans must include the finance to set up offices from the start.

Consider also that the image of the person working from home has changed a great deal in recent years. Modern technology such as faxes and e-mail, and the use of the Internet, has made it possible for some people to be in better contact with their clients than ever before without ever leaving their houses. Even large companies are encouraging their senior executives to spend some time working at home because they get more done without interruptions, and because they are just as accessible to their companies with modern technology. Such executives may even have easy access to their office 'library' material through e-mail and Internet. One of our clients, BP Amoco, actively encourages senior staff to split their time between office and home and they provide the technology necessary to operate in that way. Therefore the image of the person working at home has evolved from one of 'amateurishness' to one of 'modern professional'.

If you are the one that goes out to visit clients at their premises then it hardly matters if you have an office in the High Street or in the bedroom; they aren't going to see it anyway. Contact through e-mail is anonymous as to source; your clients cannot see the premises at which their e-mails are being downloaded. For those people whose clients contact them through the mail the addition of a 'bluff' in the address often helps. For example, for a printer to call his or her house 'Print House' in a business address will project the image of business premises and still not confuse the postman.

10

Can Anyone Challenge My Right to Be Self-Employed?

You MIGHT THINK that the question of whether or not you are self-employed is your decision to make. But that is not always the case.

The Inland Revenue make the point that to determine self-employment or employment: 'for each engagement the whole picture needs to be looked at in the light of all the facts' [leaflet IR56/NI39].

But the Inland Revenue and the Department of Social Security have a very strong determination to hold as many people in the PAYE net as possible; this means they must be classified as employees rather than self-employed. PAYE is a boost to the government's cashflow since it receives tax and National Insurance deductions each month rather than, as in the case of the self-employed, twice a year. In the past couple of years they have performed special audits in targeted industry sectors such as graphic design and the IT industry. The most recent, and largest audit of its kind, has resulted in major changes to the building industry. Many subcontractors – and many of them who should have been genuinely so classified – were forced into the PAYE net.

The force used on subcontractors was presumably legal, but it relied on creating fear. There is a section of legislation which states that it is the employer who is responsible for confirming the employment status of those they engage, and if they do not deduct PAYE where it should have been deducted then the Inland Revenue may seek to collect due taxes from the employer. Clearly no employer wanted to be put in the position of possibly being liable for his subcontractors' taxes and so followed the Inland Revenue dictat to put them into the PAYE net. There was an option offered: to approach the Inland Revenue for a ruling at the time of engagement. But the Inland Revenue seemed always to rule in favour of employment, or manage to leave a nagging doubt in the applicant's mind which was usually met with caution, and PAYE. The Inland Revenue had clearly heard of the concept 'First we must teach people to fear the law, then we can teach them to respect it.' It is possible, but by no means certain, that a future Inland Revenue may act with higher morality.

The 'Johnny Walker wisdom' that is freely given out in pubs across the land, as far as accountants can tell, is that if a person has more than one 'employer' they are therefore automatically classed as self-employed and individuals are often told to ensure that they do at least some work for one other person to protect their self-employed status. This is untrue. Although the existence of more than one person engaging you might be a factor in deciding if you are self-employed or not it is certainly not the only factor, nor the most important. It is the terms of engagement that dictate the position. So it would be quite possible to have several employers at the same time, or to be self-employed with only one client.

The general division between employment and self-employment can be summarized in the following comparison, showing the primary tools used by the authorities in determining tax status:

Employee	Self-employed
Employer works out your tax as part of a PAYE system. The employer has responsibilities to deduct the correct tax and pay it over to the Inland Revenue, also to make certain declarations each year confirming your tax position.	You are responsible for paying your own tax. Under the self-assessment regulations you are also responsible for ensuring that you inform the Inland Revenue of your profits.
Employer works out National Insurance contributions and, as above, is responsible for paying them over to the DSS.	You are responsible for paying your own National Insurance contributions.
Your own money is not at risk if the business is not successful (generally).	Your own money is at risk if the business does not succeed.

You are not responsible for profits or losses of the business (generally).	You reap the profits and suffer the losses.
You do not have an overall say in the running of the business (generally).	You make decisions and have overall responsibility for the way the business runs and the direction that it takes.
You do not set the charges for services or products sold. You are paid by time rather than assignment.	You decide how much to charge for services and products sold.
You may not have a say in the clients you are expected to work for.	You have the right to decide which clients to work for.
You operate in your employer's name.	You operate in your own name (though franchisees may not look like it!).
You may not have (and do not need) the equipment necessary to do the job; the employer provides this.	You have the equipment to do the job and are therefore a free agent, able to work for anyone who wishes to engage you.
Even if your role involves hiring people, you must hire them under your company's regulations.	You hire people under conditions you set, deciding who and who not to hire (subject to legal restrictions).
You do not have the right to substitute another person to do your job.	You do have the right to substitute another person or firm to complete your work.
If you have to 'make good' defective work you will generally be paid for the time spent.	You will probably have to correct defective work in your own time, and at your own expense.
You work at your employer's premises or where directed by the employer. (Changes in IT are resulting in many people working from home, however, who are still employees.)	You work at your own premises, though you may work at a client's premises for certain purposes.

The regulations frequently bring into PAYE people who really should not belong there, in that the regulations frighten the employers or agencies engaging temporary staff into 'defaulting' to PAYE rather than risk a battle with the taxing authorities. One acceptable way around the problem, particularly favoured by agencies who engage staff for – in particular – the building, architectural, high-tech and computer industries, is for the individual to form a limited company which then bills the agency or the client. (The Inland Revenue has recently released IR35, seeking to restrict this route.) This can, however, lead to you being on PAYE in your own company, with little saving and sometimes even more costs. In Chapter 5 we examined the merits and disadvantages of each type of vehicle through which to run your business.

It is also a 'popular' belief that once you have established yourself as self-employed, or employed, in one situation that it holds true for other engagements. This is not so. It is perfectly possible to be both employed by one business and self-employed in another at the same time. You could, for example, be a shop assistant employed by the shop during the day and running a printing business from home in the evenings and at weekends. Even when you are working in similar situations for different people it would be possible – depending on the nature of your relationship with them – to be employed by one, and self-employed in your dealings with another. Each engagement is examined on its own merits.

11 / Who Do I Have to Tell, and When?

WHEN YOU START a business you are required to tell certain authorities of the commencement. Depending on the type of business you start there are differences in the notifications required.

Unincorporated businesses

The streamlining of the government authorities has made notification of self-employment easier than ever before. One form – a CWF 1 – is available from the Contributions Agency and this notifies both the Inland Revenue and the Contributions Agency. At the time of writing this system does not always work, and having to 'chase up' the Inland Revenue is not uncommon; they usually insist that they were not notified by the Contributions Agency to whom the form is sent. This problem will change – hopefully for the better – in the near future now that the two agencies have merged.

The CWF 1 sets out its questions in two areas: personal details and business details. You will need to have this information to hand if you are completing this form, and you should ensure that you take it to your prospective accountant if you are asking him or her to complete the form on your behalf.

For personal details you are required to give:

- name (including any previous surname used)
- address
- telephone number
- date of birth

- National Insurance number (if you do not know this you can apply directly to the DSS for a notification)*
- marital status
- details of where your tax records are at present – usually based on last tax reference from a previous self-employment or from employment*

(the items marked * are usually to be found on a P45 or on a P60 from a previous or current employer; if you have such a form take it with you to your accountant)

For business details you are required to give:

- start date of business
- description of business
- business name and address (which may be your home address or business premises)
- telephone and fax numbers (it cannot be too long before an e-mail address is asked for)
- your status in the business (e.g. full owner, partner)
- if you have partners, details of them including their personal details. The partner also has to fill in an identical form.
- how you wish to pay your National Insurance contributions (see Note A below)
- if you are likely to need to defer or decline to pay National Insurance (see Note B below)
- whether you employ anyone
- if you took over the business from a previous owner; in which case give their details
- whether you are doing all of your work for one person or firm (see Note C below)
- what you were doing previously and when you ceased doing it, i.e. were you employed, unemployed, self-employed, or in education. Details will be needed; have to hand, or take to your accountant, names and addresses of your previous activities, and P45s or P60s if relevant. If you did not cease, in other words, if you are continuing to be, say, employed while running the business then information of that other activity is needed. The basic reason for these questions is to ensure that your tax and contribution files can be located and moved to the appropriate tax office.
- If you have an accountant working for you then you will also

need to give his or her details on the form, and also send a separate form (Form 64–8) which authorizes the Inland Revenue to send personal information about you to the accountant which would otherwise be confidential.

Note A
You can pay your National Insurance contributions in one of two ways. You may opt for a quarterly bill to be sent to you, or you may have the sums deducted by direct debit from your bank or building society account on a monthly basis. If you choose the direct debit option then you will need to complete a mandate form at the same time as the CWF 1 giving details of the bank account from which the amounts are to be taken.

Note B
You may not need to pay National Insurance.

If your earnings are likely to be low – profits of less than a few thousand pounds (the amount is set annually) – then you may apply for exception. You will need to obtain form CA 02.

If you already pay National Insurance contributions, if you also have employment for example, you may be able to apply for deferment. This means that you do not pay 'self-employed' contributions during the year, but that your overall earnings position is examined at each year end and any liability assessed then. The required form for deferment is CA 72B.

Note C
If you are doing all of your work for one person or firm then the tax authorities may lean towards regarding you as an employee rather than self-employed. In fact there are many other criteria involved, as described in Chapter 10. If you only have one client but are advertising for more and have a reasonable expectation of getting other work, and you have the capacity to do it, then it would be wise to point this out when submitting the form to avoid a misunderstanding by the authorities. If you are engaging an accountant, take advice on this point before completing this question on the form.

An explanation of National Insurance for the self-employed
The self-employed pay two forms of National Insurance, classes 2 and 4.

Class 4 is levied by the Inland Revenue (it is in reality a tax) and is based on profits between certain minimum and maximum limits (e.g. for tax year 1998/99 at 6 per cent between £7310 and £25,220).

Class 2 is levied by the Contributions Agency at a flat rate (for 1998/99, £6.35 per week).

Where you are not required to pay National Insurance you may choose to pay a Class 3 voluntary contribution to maintain your entitlements (for 1998/99, £6.25 per week).

The form CWF 1 also allows you to make enquiries regarding VAT registration. But this has to be applied for separately. VAT is examined below.

Notification of self-employment must be made by the 5th October following the end of the tax year (6 April to 5 April) in which the business started. Failure to do so can result in fines and penalties being levied.

Limited Companies

If you trade through a Limited Company your notification requirements are different. To own a Limited Company involves first registering one with Companies House. Most people who form Limited Companies do so through their accountant or solicitor, or through a company formation agency.

To do this you will need the following information to hand:

- *The intended name of the Limited Company.* You would be advised to have one or two 'back up' names to hand as the Companies Registry will refuse to register a name identical to, or too similar to, an existing name. You would be astonished how often it sometimes takes four or five attempts to find a suitable name! But interestingly one of our most successful clients, Bob Rontaler, MD of Goldmajor Limited, who controls 40 per cent of the amber market in the UK, was given the 'Goldmajor' name that he has since trademarked and which has been such a success 'off the shelf' from a company formation agency!
- *The intended Registered Office of the company.* This is often, but not always, the same as the trading address. For those working from home, or sometimes for other reasons, the Registered Office is often made the accountants' or solicitors'

address. Although this address must be stated on company stationery it is usually far less prominent than the trading address to where general day-to-day correspondence is sent. The Registered Office receives mail from Companies House, and is the proper address to which such legal documents as writs or summonses would be sent. The Registered Office can be changed using form 287 available from Companies House.

- Details of directors:
  1. name (including any previously used names)
  2. address
  3. date of birth
  4. nationality
  5. a description of your business occupation. (You may use this as a small piece of advertising. This information will be on public file and can be accessed by prospective clients and suppliers. Why not use this opportunity to describe your most appropriate business skills relative to the business?)
  6. the names of other companies of which the director is also a director
- Details of the Company Secretary
  1. name (including any previously used names)
  2. address
- Details of the shareholders
  1. name
  2. address
  3. the required authorized share capital (if not stated, most 'general' companies tend to have either £100 or £1000 start-up authorized share capital, divided into £1 ordinary shares)
  4. number of shares each will hold

In addition you will have to decide at some time the following information:

1. the year end of the company. Until you specify a date Companies House will appoint one. You may change it to one that suits you using form 225 available from Companies House.
2. the bankers
3. the accountants and/or auditors

Later changes can be notified to Companies House. Form 288a notifies them of additional directors or secretaries; 288b notifies them of any resignations of directors or secretaries. Form 288c notifies them of changes relating to either directors or secretaries; such as change of name or address. Form 88(2) notifies them of new shares issued within the authorized total.

It is not usually necessary to notify the Inland Revenue of your company as they receive notification of incorporations directly. They will however send a basic form for completion asking for outline details of the company and details of the directors' National Insurance numbers, etc. so that they can link their files appropriately. Directors of limited companies do not have to notify the Contributions Agency as such.

However, directors must take their salaries from the company under PAYE as employees, and therefore there is a requirement to register the company as an employer so that tax and National Insurance deducted from salaries can be paid over. This is true even if the company is a 'one-man' company with the director 'employing' only him- or herself. That said, it may be that the company does not pay salaries to anyone, even the sole director, but that the owner(s) of the business (who is probably also the sole director!) takes money out as a dividend on shares. In that case no PAYE scheme would be needed.

VAT registration

VAT is a government tax on goods and services. Whatever business you are running, self-employed or incorporated, you may have to register for VAT. Even if you do not have to, you may choose to. The procedures for both are the same.

Individuals and companies must complete a form VAT 1 *Application for Registration*. This requires:

- the name of the person or company to be registered
- the trading name if applicable
- the usual business address for day-to-day correspondence (not the Registered Office, though the two may be the same)
- the main activity of the business
- details of the nature of ownership (sole trader/partnership/ limited company, etc.)
- whether the business has been taken over from someone else

and, if so, their details and the date when you took over the business

- details of your bank account (for a Limited Company this must be the bank account in the company's name and therefore VAT registration cannot be completed until this is opened)
- details of when you started, or will start, trading and expected or actual sales figures
- prospective European Union trading figures
- details of other VAT registrations you are involved with

If the business is owned by a partnership then the partners must also complete a form VAT 2 giving individual details of the partners' names, addresses and telephone numbers.

If the business has been taken over from an already existing business then you may apply to have the 'old' VAT number transferred to you. This requires the consent of both you and the old business owners. Application is made on form VAT 68.

There are two reasons why you might register for VAT. The first is because you have to. Any business which exceeds the registration limit, usually set in the annual budget each year (£50,000 at the time of writing), must register. Failure to do so can result in fines and penalties. If you fail to register, VAT owed will be collected from you and you will be fined between 5 per cent and 15 per cent depending on the lateness of registration.

You may also register voluntarily even though you have not exceeded the registration limits. This would usually arise because:

- you had joined a franchise which required registration as part of the contract
- you sought to reclaim VAT on goods and services purchased
- anyone not registered in a business where registration would be normal would be signalling that their business does not make sales up to the registration limits, and that may be a poor piece of advertising

Take care before deciding to voluntarily register. You will then be obliged to add VAT to your prices and this may make you uncompetitive.

For example, if you are a small local builder and you would charge £1000 for a piece of work, if you are VAT registered then you will have to charge £1000 plus (at the current rates at the time of writing) £175 VAT, a total of £1175. A non-registered competitor would only have to charge £1000. If the person you are charging can reclaim the VAT the effective cost to them is £1000 either way. But if the end-user cannot reclaim the VAT – a householder for example – then you are, in their eyes, just more expensive than your competitor for the same work. This is unavoidable if your turnover is above the registration limits, but for those below the competitive edge may be what is required to build the business in the early years.

On the other hand we have encountered people who artificially hold their activities down to below the VAT limits just to avoid the bureaucracy of VAT legislation. This is surely a very simplistic and foolish approach to business. If you are concerned about the complications of VAT legislation engage an accountant to deal with it for you. Contrary to popular conception, VAT officers do not come swinging in through the windows blasting machine guns in the style of the SAS; and you have to be undertaking some very dubious tax practices to encourage them to extreme investigation. Most of the time they are very helpful with traders, a lesson that the new-style Inland Revenue will hopefully learn.

With VAT legislation it is the individual (person, partnership, or company) that is registered, not the business. So if a 'person' undertakes several trades they are all embraced by one registration. Sometimes trades that are sought to be kept out of the registration are handled through a separate entity – a sole trader who also acts through a partnership with his wife for example. But if it can be shown that the division of the business is only a device for VAT avoidance then the division can be overruled. Take professional advice before setting up such constructs.

Sensible registrations

Although not statutorily required there are also practical requirements to notify some other advisors you will need. Engage bankers, and keep them informed of your business over time. You will be forced to do so if you want to borrow from them, but this will be easier if you have built a relationship with them from the start.

You will need advice on pensions and insurances so it is wise to engage brokers and/or financial advisors early on.

You should consider the advantages of engaging solicitors in order that, when you need them, they have an understanding of your business.

We would always recommend engaging accountants from the outset, though we acknowledge the fact of vested interest in that one of the authors is a practising Chartered Accountant. Nevertheless, it is our opinion that the current tax legislation climate is one in which no self-employed person should fail to have constant professional advice on hand. One Inland Revenue District Inspector in a professional advisors training meeting commented: 'I have no doubt that self-assessment will drive clients into the arms of accountants.'

Elsewhere in the book we discuss these professional advisors in more detail.

Consider also that certain specialist areas of industry and commerce require, or advise, special registrations with related specialist bodies, for example, the Financial Services sector.

12 / Record Maintenance

IN ORDER TO comply with your requirements to complete an accurate tax return each year, including a record of income and expenditure from your business, and to pay the right amount of tax each year you need to keep a variety of records. These fall into three broad categories:

1. business documents
2. personal other income
3. capital gains information

Business documents

The law, specifically the Finance Act 1994, requires you to maintain records of your business. Failure to do so renders you liable to a possible fine of £3000. We would suggest that you keep the following documentation relating to your business:

- An analysis of all income received from all sources.
- An analysis of all business expenses incurred.
- PAYE records relating to any employees you have, including members of your family who work for you, and casual employees you engage. These records must include not just money paid, but benefits given to employees.
- Those in the construction industry need to keep records of payments to subcontractors, along with any tax deducted from payments.
- An analysis of your own drawings from the business (you are

advised to keep records of cash withdrawn, cheques withdrawn, and details of what you spent the money on).

- Loans put into the business (and where you got the loans from, what rates of interest are payable, etc.).
- Personal funds put into the business, and records of where the money has come from.
- Capital items purchased (or committed for).
- Actual receipts and copy invoices for expenditure and sales. Also, depending on the type of business, other back-up evidence of income such as till rolls.
- Bank statements for the business, together with cheque book stubs and paying-in books.
- Copies of any stocktake records. A stocktake, i.e. a physical examination and recording of stock, is usually advisable at least once a year at the year end.
- Details of any goods taken from your business by yourself or others for personal consumption. For example, if you own a food shop then you may take food for your family's own use; this must be recorded.
- Any goods or services exchanged not for money but for other goods or services supplied by someone else.
- Some evidence of the division between personal and business use of assets such as a motor car, the home telephone, etc. to enable a reasonable estimate to be made of what should be allowable for tax purposes. For the car, a mileage record of car use noting business and personal would be useful. For the telephone, an itemized phone bill is now easily available.

Such records should be maintained regularly, not just bundled together once a year. This is not just useful in presenting a case to the Inland Revenue if they enquire, but also helps you to keep 'on top of' your business and to maximize its efficiency throughout the year. We would suggest maintaining records frequently, not less than monthly and probably more frequently.

Such business records must be kept for five years from the latest date on which your tax return may be filed. So for the year 1998/99, when the tax return for 1999 must be submitted by 31 January 2000, the records must be kept until 31 January 2005. This would include the records of business entered on that tax return which could be the income and expenses for, say, the year ended 30 April 1998. If an investigation is under way, the records must be kept until that investigation is completed even if it exceeds that time period.

You are not required in law to keep a business bank account separate from your private bank account, and indeed some small or part-time businesses do not do this. However, we would recommend keeping a separate account as it is easier to maintain the business records accurately. It is also a good discipline to keep business and private finances separate in most cases. Your bank may, in any case, insist on this if they realize that you are running a business through a 'personal' account.

In addition, consider private bank and other account information, and other details of private income. Although not strictly speaking required, and indeed outside the scope of the Inland Revenue's enquiry regulations, there are times when the Inland Revenue can make assumptions you cannot displace without recourse to such papers. Unfair, and indeed draconian though it may be, it is good advice for you to keep such records while the present system exists.

Of even more concern, you may be advised to ask your domestic partner to keep their records, bank accounts and so on. The Inland Revenue positively have no right to ask for such records, but if they feel that you have failed to declare money hidden in a domestic partner's accounts then they may well undertake an investigation into them. The legality of this is questionable; but it happens, as noted in Chapter 19.

Personal 'other' income

Although this book is about self-employment, the self-employed person will probably have other records that need to be maintained. For example:

- You may also have employment, in which case keep:
- o form P60, your annual summary of earnings and tax deducted
- o copy of form P11D or P9D which your employer will give you to help complete your tax return
- o form P45 if you have left the job
- o form P160 if you have retired
- o payslips from your salary or wages
- o a summary of any tips or taxable benefits you receive
- o details of share option schemes you are involved in

o details of any Taxed Award Schemes
- You may also receive a pension in which case keep form P60 or other certificate of pension paid and tax deducted.
- You may receive taxable receipts from the government, in which case keep:
o P60 from the Benefits Agency
o details of other receipts such as state pensions, taxable benefits, statutory sick pay, statutory maternity pay, job seekers allowance, etc.
- Keep non-taxable benefit records such as child allowance as this may help to prove how you lived during the year if the Revenue question your ability to live on your stated taxable income.
- General other income:
o interest earned on deposit accounts, or other investments. Keep all records including the passbooks of buildings societies, etc.
o dividend vouchers for dividend income received, or other receipts from shares
o details of annuities received
o chargeable event certificates from life insurance payments
o details of income received from trusts
- Even though it may not be taxable keep records of other income, such as gifts or inheritances, which may be necessary to prove to the Revenue how you have supported your lifestyle throughout a period.

Capital gains information

You may make gains (rather like profits) on certain capital assets. These may typically include the buying and selling of shares; the sale of a property other than your own home (which is exempt); or the sale of valuable assets such as works of art. Tax is payable on such gains and you must be ready to prove the position.

Even if no tax is payable the income you have received will have added to your lifestyle and so you should maintain the records to show the Inland Revenue how you have lived throughout a period. This is true even of the gain you may make selling your own, exempt, personal home.

If you make losses then these losses may be available to reduce tax payments in this or future years in which case keep the records for that purpose.

There are a host of other records you may need to keep such as leases, details of trusts, foreign income, expenditures relating to child maintenance and so on. This section has covered the most typical but if you have special circumstances take the advice of a professional accountant. You may also be able to get general advice from the Inland Revenue.

Records can be kept manually or on computer (see Chapter 4). They should be kept in an orderly and well-maintained fashion. If kept on computer we would recommend keeping a back-up for safety. Indeed, a back-up at a remote location (perhaps at home if the main records are at business premises) is advisable in case of fire, flood and so on. Even if summaries ('the books') are kept on computer, the source documents should be stored safely in their original paper form, or on acceptable microfilm or similar storage.

Records other than the business records must be kept for approximately 22 months from the end of the tax year to which they are relevant. Information relating to the tax year ended 5 April 1999 must be filed by 31 January 2000 and the information kept until 31 January 2001. These time periods may be extended if the tax return is delayed.

Chapter 19 examines Inland Revenue investigations, where the records kept or demanded are seen in context.

13 / What Can I Claim For?

To REDUCE YOUR tax bill you can claim expenses against your income from self-employment. One of the most frequently asked questions during initial interviews between clients and accountants is 'What can I claim for?' In fact the real question is more like 'What can I *not* claim for?' and in this chapter you will find the rules that will let you know the claims that you can properly make for your business.

In addition, there are areas that typically get forgotten. We set out those areas to remind you to keep the right records. And the chapter includes the claims you can and cannot, should or should not, make if working from home.

General

You can claim for those items of expenditure which are used in running your business. There are two main categories of expenditure, each treated slightly differently for tax purposes.

Capital expenditure

Capital expenditure relates to the purchase of larger long-term assets of substantial value. This would typically include property, equipment, fixtures, and motor cars and other vehicles. The criteria, not precisely defined, are that:

- The item should be expected to last longer than a single accounting year. A car, for example, might be expected to usually last three or four years before being replaced.

- The item should be of reasonable size and value. Although a £2 calculator might be expected to last a number of years it would be too small and inexpensive to 'capitalize' and would therefore be written off in the year in which it was purchased (i.e. treated as 'revenue' – see below).

Capital expenditure is not directly set against the income in the year of purchase as would be the case for revenue expenditure. At the present time 25 per cent of the cost is set against profits in that year with the balance carried forward for similar relief in future years. This allowance is known as 'Capital Allowance'.

Revenue expenditure

Revenue expenditure is the day-to-day running costs of the business. Items that would typically be allowable would include:

- direct costs of materials used in the business
- labour costs of employees and subcontractors
- small equipment and replacement costs
- small repairs to equipment and premises
- rent and rates of business premises
- heat and light
- print, post, stationery
- telephone, fax, e-mail connections
- advertising and promotion costs
- vehicle running and travelling costs for business
- interest and finance charges relating to business loans and overdrafts

You can make claims for some costs that are both business and private in nature, but to do so you must calculate or estimate the business element and only claim for that proportion of the cost. For example, you can claim home heat and light over and above the normal costs you would incur in a normal domestic situation. Similarly you can claim for a telephone line at home if used for business, and for using a personal car for business.

You may not claim for your own personal expenses, such as food and holidays, or for your own drawings from a business, nor your own payments of tax and National Insurance.

You may not claim for personal insurance policies, though many business policies are allowable. The general guideline is whether it is you as an individual which benefits from the insurance (not allowable) or whether it is the business itself (allowable).

You can claim for business travel, but not for the cost of getting from your home to your place of business. Where you work from home in theory then any journey for business ought to be allowable but the Inland Revenue have occasionally challenged this and imposed an artificial concept of you 'starting work' at your client's premises. Such a challenge from the Inland Revenue should be considered for counter-challenge and legal dispute as it is often unreasonable.

There is a specific provision which disallows claims for clothing in general situations on the basis of the clothing having 'dual purpose', i.e. it could be used for both personal and business use. Arguing that you only buy suits for business and would not wear them for private purposes is not regarded as a defence. There was a case some years ago of a woman barrister, with blond hair, who argued that she was forced to wear black by the requirements of her profession but would not do so otherwise. The courts eventually rejected her claim on the basis that not to do so was a personal choice but she could do so if she wished. However, actors and other entertainers are allowed a percentage of their clothing as 'professional wardrobe', and specific items of clothing that are not regarded as having dual purpose are allowable, such as uniform clothing, special weather protective clothing, or special protective clothing for such locations as building sites (hard hats, steel capped boots, etc.).

You may not claim for entertaining clients to obtain work, though claims are available for subsistence when you are away from home, say, overnight, and for promotion providing it does not breach the rule on entertainment.

In fact, to say that these are not allowable is a reference for tax purposes. The business can in fact claim against income for all of these 'disallowable' items and it may be wise to do so in order to understand the 'true' costs of running the business. The 'disallowable' rules relate to what is allowed for tax purposes. If the business does claim these items against income then it must adjust for them in the 'tax computations' – the 'bridge' between the accounts and the taxable profits. That said, a great many businesses prepare formal accounts only for tax purposes, and may wish to disregard these costs in the preparation of the figures.

There is a popular misconception that if you claim for use of your home you will then be subject to Capital Gains Tax when you sell your home (your private residence being exempt in normal circumstances). In fact it depends on the nature of your claim. Claiming for 'revenue' items such as heat and light does not prejudice your Capital Gains Tax exemption. What might do so is if you set aside a room or part of your home exclusively for business purposes; that fraction of the home might be subject to Capital Gains Tax. The solution would be not to do it. Ensure that your 'business' area is also used by the family for other purposes, and ensure that you also use other parts of your home for working for the business.

The fact that something is eligible for offset against tax is not reason enough to fail to control that cost, though many businesses act as if that were the case. The fact that you are saving tax at, say, 40 per cent (which in effect means that you are paying 60 per cent of the cost and the government is paying 40 per cent) seems to encourage some to believe that such costs are not worth concerning themselves with. Good business requires keeping the business running at an efficient level, which maximizes income and minimizes costs at all times. Do not let allowability for tax lull you into the mistake of lacking economy. When the business is having a hard time, when cashflow is tight and the bank is refusing to honour cheques, some businessmen then start to control costs as they should have been doing all along. Think in that way at all times. They say that there is no better control over costs than to feel the 'breath of the poorhouse on your neck'!

You must consider the nature of your costs also. For example, do I want to buy premises or rent them? Do I want to buy a car, or lease one? The main difference will be in the eligibility for tax of the payments and in what year. For example, if you buy a car on hire purchase then the cost of the car is subject to capital allowances and only the interest paid each year is allowed against income. If you lease a car then you have no capital allowance claim, but the monthly lease costs are all allowable against income. (In fact cars have special treatment with restrictions on the amount that can be claimed in each year based on a notional concept of 'luxury cars' being those over £12,000 in cost – no one ever accused the Inland Revenue of being up to date with their concepts in that case!) Consider the distinction also between leases where equipment and cars are concerned; leases where you rent the equipment and not own it are 'leases' in the sense being used here. Leases where you eventually do own the item are really just hire purchase under another name.

Where you expect to make 'unusual' claims for tax purposes you should keep as much evidence for their eligibility as possible. The nature of any such cases is of course unique, but it can be explained with this example. One of our interviewees is a special effects modelmaker for the film industry. He designs and builds the spaceships used in the big blockbuster movies. Many of the parts of one spaceship he designed and built were actually from toys which he cannibalized. This individual also has young children and to put through toyshop receipts would have invited the Inland Revenue to believe that he was improperly claiming for personal items. He therefore did as we, as his accountants, advised and photographed each toy and the stages of break up and rebuild. Finally he photographed the finished model showing where the toy parts were incorporated into it. This was then presented to the Inland Revenue who accepted the claims.

Next time you are watching the blockbuster film of the year, you might try to look out for toy parts, vacuum cleaner accessories, and other cannibalized bits that are out there fighting for the Earth against alien invaders!

14 / Employing Others

For MOST PEOPLE who start up their own business there comes the important moment when you realize that you cannot do everything yourself. At this moment you have to decide either not to expand any further or to employ someone, and if growing the business is one of your goals then more people will eventually have to be taken on.

Employing others is a combination of skill, judgement, common sense and legal requirements. It's a most difficult area to get right and to some extent we must add luck to the equation.

Having decided to employ someone you are, ironically, probably the worst person to choose who and what sort of person you are looking for, because often you will be seeking a mirror-image of yourself. Even getting an interesting person to join you is made more difficult as the majority of talented people will naturally gravitate towards larger expanding companies with a known history so that they can be trained and developed and at least start a career. So the challenge is looking for a person who can work with you, or fit into a small firm, has the necessary basic skills for the job, or at least the potential to be trained, and will stay with you for the foreseeable future so as to at least recoup your recruitment and training costs.

In the short term it may be expedient to employ a fellow self-employed contractor to fill the gap until you can find the right person. However, current Inland Revenue rules do mean that if someone works solely for you for any length of time then that person may well be classified as an employee and subject to PAYE (see Chapter 7).

Where to find the right person

Strange, is it not, that when you are not looking for anybody then everybody knows exactly someone for you, and when you are looking they have all beamed up into space. So apart from personal introductions let us look at the available routes to find a suitable person.

Family, friends and relatives

Often the first choice either due to pressure from this select group or – especially for small firms with anti-social hours, e.g. shops and restaurants – one of economic necessity. Recommended only on the grounds that when you do discover they are fiddling you, at least you do not have to call the police! In truth 'loved ones' can become a difficult source for employment (how do you sack them and keep the social relationship?), but sometimes it can work very well if you make the person part of the business with sound incentives.

That said, from our experience one of the major disaster areas is employing a son or daughter. First they will comply because they have nothing better to do, or they will want to keep you happy. However, after a few months they will either wish to change your business or wreck it, and either way they will eventually walk.

Job Centres

Frankly, be wary. The staff seem not to be trained in modern interviewing techniques and are therefore unable to filter the right people to the right employments. It would be foolish not to admit the necessity of Job Centres, but while they – and those seeking work – are being used by all political parties as political footballs the system is not serving the interests of anyone well, particularly employers.

Employment agencies

With some exceptions of course, these are often an expensive waste of time. It has been said that employment agencies are analogous to children interviewing grown-ups and then charging a lot of money for giving the grown-ups your name and address.

Even more outrageous is the practice of less-reputable employment agencies in contacting a new employee they have placed with you after a few months to try and relocate them for another fat fee. We interviewed one employer who was signed up to pay a full fee (20 per cent of the employee's annual salary) if she stayed for three months; she left after three months and one day and the agency insisted no refund was possible. The suggestion was made to us that the agency had 'bribed' her to stay on to cover the period of the agreement.

Another example we had was one company who asked an agency to seek out an employee and gave them a detailed description of the type of person they were seeking. All the candidates they sent were quite inadequate for the job, and eventually the company advertised in the local press and succeeded in finding a very suitable applicant who worked for the company for several very successful years. The applicant had been on the books of the agency at the time, but they had never identified her qualities for the job.

Schools, colleges and universities

Underused and free, the employment officers at these institutions can do a really good job, if you state your requirements clearly and give them some lead time. Do remember that some of our colleges have mature students in a wide variety of skills and subjects, whose sole motive in studying is to get a good job.

Newspapers and other media

A very traditional route in trying to find the right person. The variety is legion: national press, local press, free news-sheets, trade magazines, news boards, radio, cable TV and of course the Internet. Drawbacks can be the expense, and the time and effort involved in sifting through the applications. The main advantage is that at the outset you can clearly state the type of person you are looking for and what the job entails.

Application form

Whatever route you choose to find the right person it is advisable to have an application form for candidates to fill in. The purpose of the form is to enable you to obtain factual information which can then also be used as a basis of discussion at the interview stage. The form should be kept simple and short and contain the following:

- Name, address, telephone number, date of birth, etc. This information is essential for the employee record card for the successful candidate.
- *Education*. The purpose is to consider the subjects and education chosen to see if it is a good fit with your requirements.
- *Job history*. What has the candidate done and why?
- *Interests*. Does the job you are offering give an outlet to these interests?
- *Other relevant information*. To establish economic and social stability.

Interviewing

The personnel professionals tell us that interviewing for staff is a skilful process and from our experience in large companies they do spend an awful lot of time on it. However, whatever the size of the business the basic rules appear to be the same. Remember you are looking for a win-win situation and trying to find a person who can work with you and share your enthusiasm for your business. The following guidelines should assist you in conducting a well-structured and balanced interview:

- Allow enough time for both parties to be able to explain clearly their positions. Interviews are not a race.
- Work out the questions you want to ask in advance. Have them available with the candidate's application form. Do not shoot off loads of disjointed questions that will only confuse your candidate and not tease out the correct answers.
- Ask open questions giving the candidate an opportunity to expound their best qualities. Do not ask questions that dictate the 'right' answer such as 'You have had experience of purchase chasing, haven't you?' (the desperate candidate will lie), but

rather ask questions like 'Tell me your experience in the purchasing area of the business.'

- Explain your business, your goals and what type of person you
  are looking for. Show the candidate around and discuss your
  customers/clients.
- Invite your candidate to explain previous job history. Beware
  of moths (fly high and burn out quickly), butterflies (who flit
  from job to job) and pond skaters (who only touch the surface
  of things very briefly).
- When told something by a candidate probe further to ensure
  that they really understand what they claim to understand,
  and really have had the experience they claim to have had.
  Such probing will eliminate those who have only learned how
  to conduct themselves at interviews.
- Tease out the candidate's personal values, i.e. what they hold
  dear. Self-employment is a very personal form of business and
  there is no point in employing someone whose beliefs and
  attitudes are at loggerheads with yours.
- For a customer/client-based firm seek out the person's social
  and interpersonal skills.
- Try to evaluate what makes the person tick, what is the motivation to work, and whether there is a balance, i.e. do they work
  to live, or live to work.

Ask yourself the following questions at the end of the interview, and record your answers:

- Does the candidate have the right education and skill base to
  set and deliver objectives?
- Was there demonstrated drive, energy and ambition?
- Can the person make quality decisions?
- Was the candidate at ease and responsive to change in tech-
  nology and the environment?
- Was there emotional stability and the ability to work under
  pressure and handle setbacks?
- Lastly and not least: can I work with this person?

Do not sell the candidate to yourself, particularly if you are
desperate for someone to fill the job. Be objective.

Interviewing and planning the interview is not everybody's
idea of fun, but it cannot be ignored. If possible, invite a colleague

of experience or a professional to interview with you either formally or informally. It is not a good idea to go it alone on this very important decision.

Reward money and recognition

Although people do not work for money alone, very few people work for no money at all. In large organizations money and reward systems are complex and based on many factors such as skills, education, position in the hierarchy, objectives, results and market rates. For the owner of a small business what to pay someone is not such a problem. Establishing the rate for the job is a matter for investigation and research. This can be done by referring to newspaper and trade or professional magazine job advertisements, asking around in the trade, or looking at the displays at Job Centres and employment agencies. One problem that we have identified is that self-employed people often do not pay *themselves* the going rate for the job. The reason is that some owners of a business have their living expenses subsidized, for example owners of a pub/hotel, or store may not have to pay for accommodation and/or food, drink etc. For the owner of a limited company you may well live on a mixture of salary and dividends. So remember that when you establish a rate for the job do not be clouded by what you take home in salary only. Consequently it may be necessary to pay staff more than yourself.

Non-cash rewards should be given separately from salary and benefits. Often used to recognize a particular achievement, they can range from a simple thank-you to a substantial prize. Examples of non-cash rewards are praise, peer recognition, outings, certificates, gifts, lunch or dinner, an outdoor event, i.e. ten pin bowling, time off, a training course, a press release, car parking space, a new uniform, new tools, a letter of recognition, etc. Remember the 'Christmas effect' – the effort required to choose the right gift for your employee is the same as one for your partner at Christmas. Also work out how the gift may be received. Remember the joke: 'First prize is a night out with the boss and his wife, second prize is two nights out.'

Consider profit or share schemes and bonuses. People love bonuses especially if they are unexpected or linked to a particular effort or result. The problem with regular annual bonuses is that in the minds of staff they become a right. Staff learn to expect them, which diminishes their impact. Try a 'mix and match' approach, i.e. a profit-related bonus and a special recognition one. Any bonus equation should be easy to understand and calculate. Similar to bonuses are profit related rewards. Evidence shows that in larger organizations, profit schemes can increase profits by 10 per cent. They can be used as part of a general remuneration mix, however the way the profit is to be determined and distributed must be seen to be fair and easy to calculate. Limited companies can if they so wish grant or sell shares to staff. For staff with vision and intending to stay with the firm, share schemes are a convenient way of their building up a capital sum, and at the same time being and feeling very much part of the business.

References

Having chosen the most suitable person for the job, it is essential to take up references. Preferably one reference should be work related and another as to the person's character, honesty, etc. If in any doubt at all, telephone the referee to discuss the employee.

Contract of employment

Having agreed salary, general terms and conditions of employment with your employee, and having received satisfactory references, you must within two months provide the employee with a written contract. For guidance and use standard contracts of employment are available on request for purchase from Her Majesty's Stationery Office, trade associations, professional institutes and good stationers, as well as the Solicitors Law Stationery Society Ltd. The contract of employment must include the following information:

- the name of the employer and the employee
- the date when employment began or continuous employment began
- the period of engagement, i.e. if a fixed term then when the employment will end
- the place of work and job title. It is advisable to include a brief job description

- hours to be worked and how remuneration is to be calculated, i.e. daily, weekly or monthly
- details of how any bonuses, profit or share schemes are to be calculated, if contractual
- terms and conditions of holidays and holiday pay
- termination of employment, i.e. how many weeks' notice must be given by either side
- details of grievance and disciplinary procedures
- details of trade union membership rights and collective agreements
- sick pay and leave arrangements
- details of entitlement to a company pension scheme

Should you wish to make substantial changes to a standard contract of employment then it is recommended that you take legal advice.

Employee record cards

The law requires you to keep an employee record card for each member of staff. These can be inspected by government bodies such as the Department of Social Security and the Health and Safety Executive. Similar to contracts of employment these cards can be purchased from the same suppliers. The type of record you have to keep of an employee is as follows:

- name, address, telephone number. In the event of an emergency, contact number
- personal details, date of birth, sex, nationality, criminal record if any, driving licence details if applicable to the job, and any other information that has a direct bearing on the work to be done
- health declaration, essential for food handlers and heavy physical work
- education and training record

As well as the above, the employee's file should also contain any written communications or file notes regarding the employee's employment, i.e. salary increases, change of duties/job title references, written formal warnings as well as praise and recognition letters. Dismissal and resignation letters should also be kept on file and retained.

The law also requires employers to maintain statutory sick pay records in respect of every employee being off work for more than four days together, with the days for which they have been paid statutory sick pay and days for which payments have not been made together with reasons. These records must be kept for three years.

Health and safety at work

Any small business which employs staff is advised to obtain a copy of *Health and Safety in Small Firms, an Introduction to Health and Safety* (details at the end of the book). Health and safety is about preventing yourself, your staff, contractors and visiting members of the public from being harmed at work, and also about taking the necessary precautions to make your place of business a safe place to work in. Health and safety at work applies to all firms however small as well as to self-employed people and to employees. Health and safety law is administered by inspectors from the Health and Safety Executive or a local authority. Inspectors visit work places to check that people are aware of and comply with current legislation.

All employers and self-employed people have to assess risks arising from the work place and work activities, and record their major findings of potential risks. If you employ five or more people then you are required to draw up a written health and safety policy. Employers are also under an obligation to provide health and safety training for employees and display health and safety posters at the work place. All employers and self-employed must consider, assess and record the risks and hazards that could arise at the work place. Examples given in the following list are not exhaustive.

- The use or storage of or exposure to hazardous substances such as chemicals, cleaning materials, paints, thinners and insecticides. As well as dust, fumes, bacteria, Legionella and asbestos.
- Noise pollution caused by noisy tools, machinery, engines, drills and audio equipment.
- The use and maintenance of equipment such as scaffolding, towers, ladders, machinery (guarded and unguarded), dangerous blockages, handheld tools, electrical equipment, knives, saws, hammers, lifting gear, handheld vibrating tools and drills.

- Slipping or tripping at work caused by wet or slippery floors, uneven surfaces, steps, trailing cables, badly parked or stored materials and equipment.
- Transportation at the work place, including the use of vans, lorries and other motorized vehicles, fork lift and dumper trucks and tractors.
- Fire risks due to the use and/or storage of highly flammable substances and materials such as petrol, paints, gas, dust from wood, flour and plastics, oxygen and gas cylinders.
- The internal and external maintenance of buildings, including roofs, fire exits, stairs, tanks, pits, silos, floors, internal ladders, racking and storage fixtures.
- Manual handling of materials, equipment and people. The carrying and lifting of the above, including the carrying of objects or awkward loads over long distances and over difficult surfaces.
- The use, maintenance or installation of gas and electrical equipment, overhead and underground power cables and gas pipes.
- Exposure to radiation by use of equipment such as X-ray machines, and lasers that give off ultraviolet radiation.
- The use of pressure systems such as cookers, boilers, steam heating systems and air compressors, and any equipment that contains fluids or gas under pressure.

The law requires all employers and the self-employed to be aware of and competent about what to do in the event of an accident at work, and what first aid provision must be made. In summary the minimum requirements are as follows:

- The provision and maintenance of a suitably stocked first aid box including a person nominated to be in charge of first aid, preferably with a current certificate in first aid training.
- The provision of an accident book and being aware of what to report and who has to be advised in the event of an accident.

Self-assessment

The introduction of self-assessment imposes requirements on employers to supply employees with information in good time to enable them to meet their statutory obligations to complete their tax return forms. This information includes:

- form P60 showing salary and tax deducted during the fiscal year (6 April to 5 April)
- P45 to employees who have left the company
- copies of forms P11D or P9D showing benefits-in-kind and expense payments
- details of cash equivalents of benefits-in-kind

Employers must also complete end-of-year returns (P35s and P14s) by the 19 May each year summarizing their employment totals of tax and National Insurance payable and paid. P11Ds must be submitted by 6 July each year.

15 / Insurances and Pensions

SELF-EMPLOYMENT MEANS having to manage all the administrative functions of a business and these include insurances and pensions. The insurance and pensions business, now called an industry, is part of the great financial jungle, in which there are many predators only too willing to offer advice in return for a fee or a commission. Thankfully these days professional and financial regulatory bodies are bringing a semblance of order into the law of the jungle. However, many people, as we have seen in the press and media over the last few years, have been bitten if not eaten by unscrupulous people holding themselves out to be professional advisors. Before considering any insurance or pension contract ask yourself the following questions:

- Do I need it?
- Can I afford it?
- Have I obtained alternative quotes?

Also, do not be rushed into a contract, and always beware of friends and relatives selling insurances and pensions.

Insurances

There is no mystery to insurance, the general theory of which is the pooling of risk, i.e. many people pay into a collective pot and if someone suffers loss or damage then they are paid out under the terms of the policy. Premiums are calculated on the history of claims so that if the number of motor policy claims decreases so will the insurance premiums. Most people have some insurances, normally motor car, household contents and buildings, and travel insurance when they go on holiday. So we can argue that there is a minimum necessary for day-to-day living. However, when you become self-employed often other more special insurances need to be taken out.

We interviewed an insurance broker who has a long-held view about insurance. He argues that there is a minimum insurance requirement for a self-employed person, which is based on legal requirement, i.e. motor car insurance, and on common sense relating to the lifestyle of a client and their particular business needs. To this must be added what he describes as the sleeplessness insurances, i.e. those risks actual or perceived that can keep his client awake at night, and most of these are insurable. For example if a wedding these days can cost anything between £5000 and £10,000, then a worried father and mother of the bride may well insure against bad weather ruining the reception. Let us now consider the most commonly asked questions about insurance.

What can I insure?

Almost anything is insurable as long as the person who wants insurance can demonstrate an insurable risk and an insurable interest. Therefore the manager of the Spice Girls may insure against their voices going (risk) because he would stand to lose money (insurable interest). We, as uninvolved individuals, could not insure against such an eventuality but having bought tickets to a Spice Girls gig we could insure up to the value of the tickets against the gig not being held, because we have now established risk and insurable interest.

Where can I buy insurance?

It would seem these days that insurance is widely sold. Even utility companies are now offering a range of insurance products, often through the post. The questions also pose another question as where *should* I buy insurance. This is a difficult question often depending upon your knowledge of the insurance market. For the real novice who has neither thought through insurance and indeed is bored by the whole subject the traditional insurance broker is still the best bet. Insurance brokers are specialists and although they will tell you that they are a dying breed, and that regulation and competition are killing them, the good ones seem to survive, and the newer ones entering the market are subject to examination and regulation. An insurance broker will give you advice on what insurance cover is appropriate for your type of business and will shop around for the best cover and competitive quotations. Another source of insurance products, especially life, accident, buildings and contents, are the banks. Although not independent like a broker, their advantage is simplicity. A good bank official can talk you through all your insurance needs and arrange suitable recommended insurance companies as well as their own in-house policies. You may even gain brownie points in buying insurance from the bank that conducts your business account. Insurance can also be purchased from insurance companies direct, building societies, postal offers and newspaper and television advertisements. These again are not independent advice as they are offered by a particular company. However, as we have recommended, by obtaining alternative quotes you will be in a position to compare prices.

What insurance do I need?

As previously mentioned this really has to be talked through with an insurance expert. For simplicity insurances can be divided into two main classifications, business risks and personal risks. The following list of the major insurances available are a starting point for the reader to make judgements as to what insurances are necessary and sensible for any particular business, and should help as a checklist to go through with a professional insurance adviser.

Business risks

Employer's Liability insurance

Employers have a statutory duty to insure against claims for injuries and diseases brought against them by their employees. At the time of writing the standard level of cover has been restricted to £10 million for any one occurrence, inclusive of all legal costs. The minimum level of insurance cover is £2 million. All employers are required to display a copy of the certificate of insurance at each place of business where there are employees. This insurance is usually included in a combined office policy with other insurances such as Public Liability, fire and theft for buildings and contents.

Public Liability insurance

A business must also insure against its legal liability to members of the public arising out of its occupation of its premises and carrying out its business activities. It is very similar to Employer's Liability insurance, covering accidental bodily injury to any person and accidental loss or damage to material or property. Normally the minimum recommended cover is £1 million. Again normally part of an office combined policy.

Product Liability insurance

This insurance is often an extension of the Public Liability insurance. It is designed to protect a sole trader, partnership or company against its legal liability for bodily injury, illness, disease, loss or damage to property to third parties caused by the sale of goods supplied, repaired, altered or serviced.

Professional Indemnity

This special insurance is the professional equivalent of Product Liability insurance. It covers against poor or wrong advice given by such people as accountants, lawyers, architects and management consultants.

Building and Contents insurance

As you would for your own house, then business premises and contents must be insured against various risks. Apart from the standard risks of fire, theft, storm and explosion, policies are usually extended to 'all risks' which will then cover special perils such as malicious damage, flood, burst pipes, impact by road or rail vehicle, earthquake and civil commotion. If you rent your business premises then your landlord is usually responsible for insuring the building, and your proportion of the cost will be reflected in the rent. You will still be responsible for all the plant, machinery and contents. If you lease equipment or are buying it on hire purchase you must make sure that each item is insured and your cover is adequate. Depending on the building and the type of business you are conducting then some types of property may need special mention and cover by your insurance company, e.g. cash in transit, computers, hardware and software, glass windows, goods in transit, etc. Building and Contents insurance can form part of an office combined policy.

Motor insurance

Most people are conversant with motor car insurance and similar rules apply to lorries and vans. The law requires a minimum of third party risk although comprehensive cover is always to be recommended especially for business use. If you own a number of vehicles then fleet discounts are available from the insurance companies. Heavy goods vehicles require special insurance consideration and specialist advice will need to be taken.

Goods in Transit insurance

If you are in the business of sending, moving or transporting goods by rail, road, Post Office (Parcelforce) or private carriers for the UK and/or international carriage then often insurance is available by the carriers at competitive rates. However, Goods in Transit insurance is recommended for businesses who use their own or hired vehicles. Motor vehicle policies do not normally cover such goods. Premiums are calculated by the method of conveyance, the nature of the goods, how it is packed and in what, previous claims experience, where the goods are going and the value.

Credit insurance

There is no substitute for an efficient credit control system, which includes careful research of a customer before granting credit, and making sure that your customer pays you on due dates. In many businesses, particularly self-employed firms, debtors are the largest asset, and non-payment of debts is one of the main reasons why small businesses fail. You can insure against bad debts in two main ways. You can insure against all your customers going broke, the premium being calculated on your gross turnover, or more cost effectively you can insure specific customers. Obviously they will be the largest and more high-risk ones, the premium being calculated on the customer's history and/or the percentage of your turnover that customer represents. For export sales then the government provides an export credit insurance, details of which can be found at the government's Export Credit Guarantee Department.

Fidelity insurance

If you employ staff then it is possible to insure yourself against the risk of financial loss as a result of fraud and acts of dishonesty by your employees. You can negotiate a general policy which covers all employees without naming them, although different premiums usually apply to different categories of employment or risk, e.g. telephonist rather than bank cashier. Or you can arrange individual policies on selected employees, identified by name and the position they hold in your business. If necessary you can insure the position rather than the name. Premiums will depend on the degree of risk but in order to keep premiums down sensible safeguards can be put in place, e.g. restriction of cheque signing powers, minimizing cash handling, internal audit systems, the correct taking up of references, and the safe storage of movable valuable items.

Partners/Shareholders Protection Assurance

If uninsured many small businesses face difficulties when a partner or major shareholder dies. It is therefore a good idea to arrange Partners/Shareholders Protection Assurance that can be taken out by partners/shareholders to provide funds for surviving partners/shareholders to pay for the shares of the deceased. Also Key Person (i.e. someone important to the running of the business) Insurance can be taken out by companies who stand to lose financially by the death of a key person.

Loss of Profits insurance

If your business cannot continue in the short term due to an insurable risk, i.e. fire, theft, flood, etc., then you may not be necessarily insured against loss of profits. Loss of Profits insurance will pay you the shortfall until the business is back to normal trading conditions. As the premium will be calculated on your profitability as shown in your accounts, it is often difficult to arrange this type of cover until you have a proven track record. In this case it is possible to insure the risk of additional expenses incurred by arranging increased cost of working cover.

One joke within the insurance industry is the self-employed person who takes out all the insurances he can, such as fire, theft, etc., but refuses flood insurance. When asked why he said 'What good would it be? How on earth can you start a flood?'

Other risks

As we said at the beginning of this chapter most risks are insurable, and the insurance industry does offer cover for special risks such as terrorist damage cover, third party computer fraud, commercial legal protection and many more which can be discussed with your insurance adviser.

Travel insurance

If you are travelling for business, then it is advisable to arrange travel cover for you and your employees who are also required to travel, e.g. sales persons. These policies are easy to arrange and the premiums are normally calculated on the number of trips undertaken per year and the destinations. One advantage of annual travel insurance packages is that they can often be extended to include holiday travel as well.

Personal risks

Life assurance

Being self-employed means that in the event of your death your estate will have to settle your business as well as private affairs. If you have a family then they will need to be protected against claims upon your estate as well as loss of your earnings. Most people have a very good understanding of life assurance, what is available, and what it costs, of course depending on age and health history. As a rule of thumb the amount of cover you need can be calculated by the following simple formula:

Business debt + Personal debt + (3 × net income after tax)

Obviously 3 × your net income after tax is an arbitrary figure and a matter for personal choice.

Personal Accident Insurance

Personal Accident Insurance is relatively cheap but it can often depend upon your trade or profession. An office-bound accountant will not be marked as such a risk as a self-employed scaffolder. Personal Accident Insurance can often be included as part of an office combined policy or annual travel insurance. In view of the low cost it is worth taking out for higher risk trades such as the building and construction industry, or self-employed oil rig and oil platform workers.

Critical Illness and Income Protection Insurance
As we have said, being self-employed means that you take all the risks. One of the risks is falling critically ill, so that you may not be able to continue working. Funds permitting this type of 'cushion' may well enable you to sleep better at nights. Competition in this market has recently driven the rates down, and it is well worth shopping around.

Private Health Insurance
The 1997 year end figures for the National Health Service were not good reading. The waiting list was 1,260,000 patients or 1 in 40 of the population. Patients waiting for hospital treatment for more than a year were 70,000. As is so often in life, the alternative to depending on the state is to make your own provision, and private health insurance is available in many different levels of innovative cover, ranging from fully comprehensive to basic hospitalization treatment only. The great advantage for self-employed people is that you can get treatment quicker, at the dates of your choosing, as well as picking your own specialist. This results in less disruption of your business. Remember you are not paid when you are off sick. However, this insurance is not cheap and becomes more expensive as you get older.

Good practice

- Always obtain alternative quotes.
- Deal only with reputable and registered companies.
- Read the policy documents including the small print very carefully however boring it may seem.
- Do not spend money on non-essential cover.
- Review all your insurances once a year with your adviser.
- On proposal forms you must disclose all the material facts.
- In any dispute use the free services of the Insurance Ombudsman – see Useful Addresses at the end of the book.

Pensions

The problem with pensions are that they are not a problem for the young, they are only half a problem for the middle-aged, and a considerable problem for people about to retire. Our view is that you can never be too healthy or have too many pension arrangements. Self-employed people are by nature optimists and we have met many who defer making pension arrangements, taking the view that 'my business will be successful and then it will look after me, or I can always sell it'. These people are heading for a poor retirement. Our advice for the self-employed is that you can never start a personal pension scheme early enough. The national opinion poll carried out a study of pensions for a major clearing bank and some of its findings were:

- The minimum amount of pension needed for a comfortable retirement (at time of writing) is argued to be £9300 p.a. or £179 per week. This is equal to only half the national average earnings.
- 20 per cent of the population is projected to have a pension of 50 per cent of the national average earnings when they retire.
- Some 13 million people are going to retire on about £120 per week.

At present (time of writing) the state provides a basic pension of £64.70 per week, which is under a fifth of national average earnings, and considering the national debate going on about pensions, only a true born optimist would consider retiring on the state pension. Self-employed people must therefore make their own private pension provision, and personal pension policies for the self-employed have been available since 1988.

Personal pension plans are provided by insurance companies and commercial firms including some well-known retailers. An independent financial advisor's advice is best sought and it is prudent to invest in more than one provider in order to spread the risk. Personal pension plans are very flexible and can offer the following:

- You can pay the premium monthly, quarterly or annually and the premiums can be changed depending upon your financial circumstances.

- You can invest a lump sum as and when you like which is a convenient way of using your income tax relief on pension contributions as and when profitability permits.
- At the termination of the pension plan period, usually between your 50th and 75th birthday, you will be able to shop around for the best available annuity (open market option).
- You can choose to take a lower amount of pension with a tax free lump sum.

As a self-employed person, contributions to a recognized pension plan are allowable for tax relief at your highest rate, therefore if you are paying tax at 40 per cent a lump sum contribution of, say, £5000 will only cost you £3000. At the end of the pension plan period the funds must be used to purchase an annuity, i.e. funds remaining after your lump sum allowance. An annuity is in effect a gamble on your life. At the time of writing a pension fund of £100,000 for a man of 60 will purchase an income of £8000 p.a., less if you purchase an annuity with inflation built in. Annuity rates rise and fall in line with the yield on long-dated gilts and again, at the time of writing, annuity rates are low so now may not be a good time to retire. However, buying an annuity can be deferred and instead you can draw down from your pension funds until age 75. The advantages are that your pension fund remains fully invested which gives you the chance to buy an annuity on better terms later, and the benefits on early death may also be better. You can vary the income you wish to draw off the fund and the tax free lump sum is still available to you. This arrangement is not suitable in every case and advice should be obtained.

Regarding tax relief the government restricts the percentage of your income allowable for tax relief and these are as follows:

Age of the start of the tax year	Percentage of income allowable for tax relief
35 or less	17.5
36–45	20
46–50	25
51–55	30
56–60	35
61–74	40

When choosing a personal pension provider it is good sense to get competent impartial advice, so that a plan can be drawn up that gives you the flexibility to allow changes depending on your financial circumstances. Remember mistakes are very costly in this industry.

16
Professional Advisors

SELF-EMPLOYED PEOPLE, unlike managers in large companies, do not normally have in-house professional advisors. From the start of your business and as it grows, you cannot avoid coming into contact with, or using the services of, such people. In Chapter 15 we considered pensions and insurances, both of which need independent advice; similarly from time to time you will need advice from other professionals, e.g. bankers, accountants, lawyers, etc. They in turn may refer you to another platform of advisors, e.g. a solicitor may refer you to a patent agent for your new invention, or an accountant may refer you to a tax barrister when you have made your first million. Professional advisors are highly trained experts in their own field, and as such are expensive and should only be used sparingly. Never be intimidated by them, and as situations arise when you feel you do need professional advice it is worth investing in a preliminary discussion right at the outset rather than trying to go it alone, which in our experience is often an expensive mistake.

Bankers

Banks have a bad press. A bank manager of the old school informed us that the reason was that due to the 'grab a customer policy' of recent years, people who would not have been entertained previously were given bank accounts. He also concluded that we now have a generation of young people who, influenced by their parents and the media, treat banks with no respect and view bank managers as a cross between Dad's Army and a second-hand car salesman. This view is further aggravated by ill-informed financial and television hacks who either do not understand what banks do or have no wish to. It is not our job to defend banks and we all know mistakes can and do happen, but as a very senior executive of a High Street bank once told us, 'often we are only asking for our money back'. For the self-employed business person the help and assistance of a good bank manager is an essential part of the business plan. Bank managers tend to lend to people, so a comfortable working relationship helps especially when you need help to see you through a rough patch. So what exactly can the banks offer the self-employed business person?

Generally people think of banks as institutions that will operate your cheque account, give you an overdraft to finance trade fluctuations of, say, stock and debtors, and grant you medium or longer term loans to finance assets such as buildings, plant and machinery, vehicles and equipment. Of course this is the stock in trade of the High Street banks, but they also offer a raft of other services such as advice on investments, import and export documentation, insurances, pensions, wills, mortgages, factoring debts, business plans, and all the other products and services expected of large financial houses. Banks also collect and refine economic data, and provide it to customers in the form of information fact sheets.

Choosing a good and helpful bank is not as difficult as it sounds. The secret is research and shopping around. Ask around and listen to the stories of help and of woe. Most of the High Street banks now have specialist small business managers who are dedicated to looking after and assisting people starting up in business, and helping their business to grow. We have found either from personal experience or from talking to our clients that it is not the bank, nor even the branch, that makes the all-important difference but rather the character of the individual manager in charge of your account. A good relationship with a professional manager can make business-running much smoother than it would otherwise be.

From our own and our clients' experience, banks are never a problem if you stick to your agreement with them, and if you do wish to go over your authorized borrowing limits, then this in the first instance is not usually a problem as long as you consult with them and keep your bank manager well-informed, as well as providing the financial and other information asked for. It should be borne in mind that banks have a long history and an even longer memory. When you submit your business plan to the bank expect it to be analysed against a historical and deep database. Over-optimistic targets and profit projections will be compared and tested against people in similar businesses to your own. Trying to con a bank manager is unproductive and hurts your reputation. In choosing a bank and establishing a working relationship we recommend the following:

- Open an account only with a reputable bank, i.e. any High Street bank. Discuss with the manager what interest rates they charge for borrowing and how they structure their transaction charges.
- If you decide to open an account at a business centre, arrange drawing facilities at their nearest branch to your place of business – essential if you are having to transport cash.
- Keep your bank manager fully informed at all times of any change in your circumstances that impacts upon your business and/or your general finances.
- Meet your bank manager at least twice a year to review your borrowing requirements and your business plans.
- Overdrafts are for financing the peaks and troughs of your cashflow, not for financing fixed assets which should be financed through medium- and long-term loans.
- Always furnish your bank manager with the financial information required, i.e. quarterly trading results, stocks, debtors and creditors.
- Negotiate the lowest interest rate possible. Remember that banking is highly competitive and they want your business.
- Resist strongly giving personal guarantees on your house. Most banks will accept a charge over the assets of your business.
- If you strike up a really good relationship with your bank manager, and he or she moves branch, it might be sensible to move your account there as well.
- But do not hop from one bank to another on a whim. A new manager may not support you as well as one who has had a long-term working relationship with you.
- Do not give one bank all your business. When it comes to your review time managers do look at their total exposure to you, for example, overdraft, medium- and longer-term loans, credit

cards. Spread your business about. This will increase your options if you need to re-sort your financial arrangements.

Banks are there to give all sorts of financial and business advice. However, do not be on the phone too regularly to your manager as most charge for each contact made.

Banks are also conduits for government-led initiatives such as enterprise schemes, management of grants, start-up loans, etc. For this reason they are a most useful first point of contact in investigating what financial assistance may be available to you. Finally there is no merit in breaking the bank's rules or breaching their agreed limits with you. Bank managers talk to other managers of all financial institutions, and electronically they can render your credit rating worthless, or cancel loans and mortgages and other facilities.

Lawyers

In our experience any contact with lawyers is expensive. In the City of London solicitors' fees are between £200 and £300 per hour. The cardinal rule is that if at all possible never involve legal people in legal matters. Most self-employed people run smaller businesses and can find themselves vulnerable to pressure from large organizations, institutions and government departments, especially in relation to debt collection, contracts, or new rules and regulations. So, in some circumstances it is going to be unavoidable to consult lawyers, and the following guidelines and notes are offered from our own past and sometimes costly experiences:

- In choosing a solicitor three main routes are available to you – recommendations from friends or business contacts, advertisements placed by solicitors in the press, or contact with the Law Society, who will send you a list of practitioners in your local area.
- Most solicitors belong to a scheme whereby they charge a set nominal fee for an initial consultation of usually an hour's duration. During the initial meeting establish their expertise and experience in the legal field that you wish to consult on.
- Agree a budget and target dates with your solicitor at the outset, or else correspondence will ebb and flow between the parties as

timeless as the Nile. See if your solicitor is prepared to take on the case on a no-win no-fee basis.

- Always ask your solicitor's view on litigation. A friend of ours, who is a leading specialist in computer law, argues that going to court is a defeat for both parties. Definitely never go to court on a point of principle. Remember the legal maxim 'Never take a man of straw to court', you may win the principle but your pockets will be lighter.

- Beware of your solicitor recommending taking counsel's advice. This is always a very lengthy and expensive process.

- Some basic legal work can often be done by yourself, for example purchasing standard contracts of employment or, partnership agreements from the Solicitors Law Stationery Society, or at least being well-prepared before meeting your solicitor.

- Some business transactions by nature of their complexity most definitely need the benefit of legal advice, e.g. the purchase or sale of buildings, businesses, franchise operations, complex loan or other financial instruments, as well as the acquisition or sale of other major assets.

- As mentioned in the chapter on insurances and pensions, where possible for identifiable and regular risk it may be possible to insure against the need to take legal advice.

- Finally, explore all the available avenues of settling a legal dispute such as arbitration, ombudsmen, regulators, etc. before sailing down the legal river.

The best depiction of the legal system we have seen was a cartoon with two farmers fighting over each end of a cow while a lawyer sat in the middle, milking it.

Accountants

Being self-employed does not necessarily mean you need to have an accountant. This will depend on how confident you feel in drawing up a set of accounts for the Inland Revenue, compiling and submitting your own income tax returns, how complex your financial transactions are and whether you can actually be bothered to deal with the above. Accountants are not necessarily expensive, and we take the view that a good accountant should at least save you their fee, by offering up to date and sound advice. The migration from manual book-keeping systems to inexpensive accounting software packages does mean that self-employed people can produce a very workable set of accounts without necessarily understanding book-keeping. The best use of accountants is for putting a set of accounts to bed, submitting them on your behalf to the appropriate people and for offering proactive advice on running your business more efficiently, and profitably. Choosing an accountant is similar to choosing a solicitor, except that there is often a closer relationship with the accountant who will, after all, know all your financial ins and outs year after year. In many cases the relationship of a client to an accountant is not far off that with his or her doctor; and you need to be able to confide in them. For this reason it is as well to strike up a good and open friendly working relationship.

Choosing and working with your accountant includes the following:

- Most small accountancy practices get work by personal recommendation from existing clients, so do some research and ask around your business contacts and friends, etc.
- When interviewing an accountant establish their professional qualifications. You will wish to know if they specialize in small businesses and what experience they have in the field you are in.
- Most accountants these days will negotiate a fixed fee with you reviewed annually and explain how their charging system works. Please bear in mind, however, that they will charge for work extra to their original brief.
- Clearly agree what work you are responsible for (e.g. preparing accounts to trial balance, producing draft Profit and Loss Accounts and Balance Sheets) and what work you expect your accountant to do.
- Always remember that your accountant is on your side, and is not a fifth column for the Inland Revenue and VAT authorities.
- Always be totally open and honest with your accountant, and appreciate that if you disclose information of a sensitive nature they may be professionally obliged to act upon it.
- Your accountant is there to give you proactive advice, not to always react to good or bad news. Do not spring surprises and if you see trouble ahead in your business or indeed personal circumstances, do consult and ask for advice.

Accountants do have an unfortunate image in the UK. Some of the blame can be directed to the Monty Python shows of the 1970s, representing them as dull and boring. Also in industry and commerce it is common to hear of accountants referred to as bean counters, hatchet men, etc. But accountants do not only count the money and for the self-employed they can be the 'one stop shop' for general advice on accounts, information technology, income tax, VAT, National Insurance, employment law, company formations, company taxation, and secretarial work as well as financial advice on hire purchase and leasing agreements, banking arrangements and business plans. You will find that experienced small business accountants do understand your business, and can give you professional unbiased advice based on their dealings with people in similar positions to yourself.

Grants, Help and Support Available

THERE ARE MANY, many grants available for businesses. It is, however, one of the real minefield areas which frankly has not been addressed well by the government. What is needed is one government body which either administers all grants or, more usefully, co-ordinates and distributes information on grants throughout the country. Small businesses could apply to that body for information, setting out their position and asking for advice. Unfortunately, such a body does not exist. What actually exists is a whole load of private and government organizations, at both national and local level, all of which have some information. But the picture is very confusing. Obviously the Department of Trade and Industry is the major step closest to the ideal, but it has not yet embraced the full picture. They mostly concentrate, reasonably enough, on those grants they themselves administer.

And it is about time that a government umbrella was constructed for this purpose. A Japanese report in the summer of 1998 states that of all the commercially valuable inventions exploited in Japan since 1945, 55 per cent had been invented in Britain. Most had been ignored in Britain and had had to go abroad for support. The loss to Britain in finance and prestige is horrifying.

The EU has been at the front of promoting grants in many areas of activity to ensure that Europe maintains a place with other world-leading areas such as the United States, but as you might expect with the EU, bureaucracy and complexity is the name of the game.

One of the real problems is that most grants are not available in retrospect. If you employ someone and then apply for a subsidy grant it will probably be too late; you have to apply, then employ.

This section, then, sets out the 'dos' and 'don'ts' that might be helpful, and a general summary of the areas in which grants might be available. It cannot be more specific; the only thing more changeable than the types of grants available is the English weather. You must follow the 'dos' and 'don'ts', talk to your professional advisors such as your accountant, your bank, and your local business services such as Business Link, the Chamber of Commerce or the Department of Trade and Industry, and try to think ahead of your own needs as to what might, at the time, be available.

Do

- Study every project or aspect of change in your business and proposed business and ensure that you have discussed every such aspect with advisors and the local business community.
- Seek out grant-giving bodies and, even if you are not yet ready to make changes that the grant would apply to, ask for details of how – and at what stage – application should be made.
- Try to get a working relationship with someone in the grant-giving body. You will need friendly advice.
- Have ready your detailed business plan (as examined in Chapter 8) to submit to the bodies as required. Ensure that it includes detailed explanations of the use of the grant if it is offered.
- Be thorough in completing the application forms. Grant-giving bodies are notorious about 'dotting the i's and crossing the t's'. Your relationship with someone in the body will help here.
- Maintain contact with the grant-giving body and ensure that your application does not get lost in the bureaucracy.

Don't

- Don't expect to get a grant for something you have already paid out for or started. Generally grants must be applied for before the event.
- Don't be a nuisance to the grant-giving body, or try to put

pressure on them. Maintaining contact with them (above) is intended to mean a positive, business-like contact.

- Don't play grant-giving bodies off against each other. They do have contacts with each other and don't take kindly to such attitudes.
- Don't lie and try to get grants you are not entitled to. You will almost certainly end up committing fraud. The bodies are generally very keen to police their activities; they will probably prosecute.
- Do not pay money 'up front' to the variety of often dubious schemes that will flood your letterbox offering to find grants for you. Most will take your money for nothing, some will give you a hand-out of information and leave you to do the work, and many you will never hear from again. There is, in any case, no need to do this; contact your Local Business Link for advice both on grants available and the reputable local assistance you can call on.

What sort of grants are available?

Energy

There are grants available to promote the development of new energy measures and efficiencies, and to promote the application of proven good practice in energy efficiency.

Rural development

Grants can be available for building refurbishment and for improving rural transport schemes.

Food processing and marketing

Substantial grants are available in this field but at present only in Scotland, Wales and Northern Ireland.

Employment

Grants of many sorts are available to relieve unemployment, particularly in recognized depressed areas where major infrastructures have collapsed, for example areas which used to be supported by coal mining, steel manufacture, and the defence industry hit by the so-called 'peace dividend'.

Research and development

Grants are available for the development of new technologies and for researchers in many scientific fields. The two main government grants are presently SMART and LINK. Keep up to date with this area through your local Business Link, or the Department of Trade and Industry.

Creativity

The arts and entertainments are supported by a variety of grants, mostly to aid start-ups.

Import and export

The UK has always been keen to promote export and grants are available for businesses wishing to expand their markets abroad. But importers have not been ignored and some grants are available for them too.

Joint ventures

The EU is keen to promote joint venture work across national boundaries and grants are available for many kinds of such activities. They include joint ventures between EU member states, between the EU and the members of the former Soviet Union, and for joint ventures in Latin America, Asia, South Africa and other selected parts of the world.

Local work

The numbers of local grants available are almost endless, dealing with crime prevention, local venture initiatives, the development of co-operatives, local employment initiatives, and more. Again, your best local source of information is your Business Link.

If you cannot locate your local Business Link address directly you will be able to do so through your bank or your accountant.

18 / Self-Assessment

THE NEW SET of rules for the self-employed has been heralded as the greatest change to the tax system for over a hundred years. And so it is. Modelled on the much-feared American system, it imposes huge responsibilities on the taxpayer and despite the 'cosy' image of the Inland Revenue's cartoon figure 'selling' the changes to the public, it has also been described as 'an iron fist in an iron glove'. One Inland Revenue officer stated: 'All we have to do is send out the forms and then collect the penalties.' The change to the system was announced by the then Chancellor of the Exchequer in March 1993 and commenced with the Finance Act 1994.

Many people – taxpayers and practitioners – believe that the actual imposition of self-assessment is somewhat at odds with the Revenue's statements. For example, it is unquestionably more complicated given that the Revenue have effectively divested themselves of any responsibility to advise taxpayers, yet the Inland Revenue state that this ' . . . will simplify the tax rules for millions of people'. To judge the position consider the 'before' and 'after' rules on residency. For some employees it is a matter of complication to decide in which country they are resident, which affects their tax status. Before self-assessment the Revenue would look at the facts and issue a 'ruling' which would enable the taxpayer to plan for, and make payment of, the right amount of tax. Under the new self-assessment rules the Revenue refuse to give such rulings and leave it to the taxpayer to 'take his or her best shot', to pay what they believe is right, and then suffer penalties and interest if the Revenue afterwards decide they view the matter differently. Although there are few such clear-cut examples facing the self-employed, many such people who have traditionally dealt with their own accounts and tax returns are coming to accountants complaining that they now feel they need professional advice, partly because the system has become more complicated and partly because they cannot get useful advice any more from the Revenue.

It is true to say that there is a certain simplification in that the 'self-assessment' tax return and tax payments now embrace all taxes in a once-a-year declaration and in combined payments rather than the various pay dates and assessments that used to be raised.

The most significant effect is on the self-employed. They have all the responsibilities and duties not only to maintain their records, as before, but to calculate and pay taxes due on time without the prompting of the Inland Revenue. Failure to do so can result in heavy fines and penalties. The Inland Revenue have far fewer responsibilities to the taxpayer.

The Inland Revenue have also stated that they believe that self-assessment would be less confrontational than its predecessor (SAT2–1995). That has not, to date, turned out to be true though it is still early days for the system and the Inland Revenue are certainly having their difficulties while the system beds down. Nonetheless relationships between the Inland Revenue, taxpayers and the professional accountancy bodies have probably never been so strained. At one lecture evening in 1998 where the Inland Revenue presented a review of the first year of self-assessment to members of the Institute of Chartered Accountants (where one of the authors was present) there was a feeling of real hostility, question time was certainly not 'less confrontational', and what would usually in the past have been a good-humoured exchange with a degree of banter began to look like the Somme the day after a bad night in the trenches.

The Revenue argue that taxpayers' '. . . contact with the Revenue will be reduced to a minimum' by the system. This is not so. Under the old system most taxpayers would go through their whole business lives without more than general administration with the Revenue. Now, under the new system of investigations, it is likely that on average within a ten-year time span every taxpayer will be investigated – a massive increase in Revenue contact and of a nature the taxpayer is unlikely to welcome.

The key to the system is in a major change to the processes

employed by the Inland Revenue. Under the previous system the Inland Revenue administered the taxation system. They would take submissions of figures from taxpayers and process bills to send them. If the bills were wrong the Inland Revenue were responsible, unless of course they had been misled by the taxpayers. Under the new system the taxation system is administered by the taxpayers themselves. They submit not just figures, but calculations of tax payable. They have to pay their taxes without the Inland Revenue's prompting. If the taxpayer pays the wrong tax then the Inland Revenue charge fines and penalties.

Although the Revenue can argue that they offer the option of them calculating the tax liability if the return is submitted before 30 September each year, this is somewhat disingenuous. The calculation is just an arithmetic exercise based on the data provided. The data provided still comes from the taxpayer, and that is where all the potential for error remains – where the Inland Revenue have no responsibilities. The Revenue even admit this within their document *Self Assessment – The Legal Framework* (SAT2–1995): 'All such "Revenue calculations" will subsequently be treated as if they were self-assessments. So these calculations should simply be regarded as assistance provided by the Revenue to help taxpayers self-assess.'

Since the taxpayer is virtually deprived of advice and rulings from the Revenue – and in fact professional advisors are largely so deprived also – there is inevitably going to be an increase in fines and penalties where the Revenue, after the event, challenge the tax paid. This 'back-door' taxation stands to increase the Treasury's cashflow considerably. After the first self-assessment deadline of 31 January 1998 for submission of the first self-assessment tax return it was said that around a million people were late. If so, then at £100 fine per return that could yield £100,000,000 pounds extra for the Revenue in that year alone (source: *Money Mail*, 4 February 1998). Add to that a second batch of fines months later, and surcharges for late paid tax, and it is clear that this is a major new source of funding for the government.

The morality of such a system could be, and has been, questioned. But the fact is that unless the system is reformed the self-employed have to live with it. And it is unlikely to be reformed within eight to ten years in our opinion. The present New Labour government inherited the system from the outgoing Conservative administration and can reasonably argue that it wasn't their creation, and that it takes several years to test a system until it is modified. Such tests should take it, with its attendant very useful increased finances, to the end of the second period of office which it seems set to be elected to.

One of the consequences of the system is to remove a massive amount of administration from within the Revenue. They no longer have to do anything other than process returns sent in and trigger computer 'dumps' of tax calculations and tax statements periodically. This is a huge saving to the Inland Revenue, with their work now being done by the public at no cost. In the same manner as with VAT, each self-employed individual is now an unpaid tax administrator and collector for the government. The Inland Revenue staff are therefore released to be able to conduct investigations. Whereas in the past perhaps one per cent of taxpayers were investigated, now nearer to ten per cent are likely to be so treated. (The Revenue have stated that there is a target of 800,000 enquiries likely in the tax year, against 8 million self-employed.) The Revenue have even enshrined in law what they have had to do 'by the back door' in the past; they can randomly check individuals without having any cause or evidence to show. Such activities by the police in communities of ethnic minorities – the so-called 'suss' laws – were suppressed by law years ago; unfortunately the predominantly perceived middle-class activity of running a business has not come to the attention of civil rights groups. The Revenue argue that '. . . we will also make some enquiries about returns which do not seem to have anything wrong with them. This is to ensure that the system is operating fairly and properly . . .' (IR 142). What they do not say is that for six months to a year the taxpayer will live under the stressful threat of prosecution for having committed no crime and could end up paying tax they should not have to pay in order to 'test their system'. Investigations are examined in Chapter 19.

The new system does of course have some advantages to the self-employed and these are to be welcomed:

- Tax is assessed on the current year basis rather than the complicated preceding year basis of the old system, so tax is payable nearer to the time the profits are being earned.
- The payments on account demanded by the Revenue are based

on the previous year's liability and therefore at any time an accurate schedule for up to two years ahead of payments to the Revenue can be calculated. This allows taxpayers to plan their finances better. (The system provides a permanent cashflow advantage to the Revenue too!)

- Partnerships are no longer taxed as a body. The tax falls on the individuals as part of their overall annual summary.

Penalties

If tax returns are submitted late there are penalties to face. Tax returns must be submitted at the latest by 31 January in the year following the year of issue. So the tax return in 1999 covering income for the year ended 5 April 1999, which is issued in the early weeks of April 1999, must be returned by 31 January 2000. (Late issued returns are due back later, three months after issue. But a word of warning: the fact that you did not receive a tax return does not mean that when you ask for one and it is issued this delay applies. The Inland Revenue tend to claim that the return was issued in April and must therefore have gone astray. They are not required to prove that one actually was issued.)

A late delivered return incurs a fine of £100 and a further £100 fine if the return is still not delivered six months after the due date.

The Inland Revenue have also reserved powers to fine individuals £60 per day for late submissions of returns.

A tax-based penalty can also be imposed, doubling the true tax liability for the year, if the return is still outstanding one year after the due date.

Partners in partnerships are all subject to these penalties if one partnership return is sent in late. There are no tax-based penalties however as these are imposed on the individual partners.

Interest is charged on penalties paid late.

The Revenue will look at a 'reasonable excuse' for late submissions. These, they say, might include:

- Non receipt of a tax return if the taxpayer can prove he or she did not receive it.
- The tax return not reaching the Inland Revenue due to fire, flood or industrial action at the Post Office.

- Loss of business or tax-required records due to fire, flood or theft at your premises, if you can prove the circumstances.
- Serious illness such as coma, stroke or major heart attack (yes – they actually state 'major'!).

Surcharges and interest

Surcharges are imposed on late payments of tax. Tax payments under self-assessment are due on 31 January and 31 July each year. A 5 per cent surcharge is imposed on tax paid more than 28 days after it is due, and a further 5 per cent charged if the payment is still unpaid six months after it is due. The surcharges are actually imposed only on final payments, not payments on account (which form the majority of most of the 31 July payments).

Appeals are based on 'reasonable excuses', which the Revenue state could include:

- cheque lost in the post if you could prove it
- bank error
- serious illness (as noted above – don't forget to make your heart attack 'major'!)

Surcharges are in addition to interest, which is charged on all late payments on a daily basis.

Companies

Companies will come into a version of self-assessment, called Corporation Tax Self-Assessment, for the year ending on or after 1 July 1999. The impact of the move to this system will not be as great as for individuals, as the existing system for companies was virtually a hybrid of the old and new systems anyway. In order to complete accurate accounts companies have always had to compute their tax liability based on their profits each year.

19
Tax Investigations

THE INLAND REVENUE have acquired sweeping powers to investigate all aspects of your business and personal life. And, frankly, under the new regime within the Inland Revenue these powers are being used by Revenue Officers in ways that seem to us to border on the improper. You will be inconvenienced and distracted for months, and sometimes years, by such scrutiny.

We are forced to wonder at the message intended by the government in naming their cartoon taxman, who has been advertising self-assessment on television since the summer of 1995, 'Hector'. *The Concise Oxford Dictionary* defines 'hector' as 'a bully; to bully, to intimidate'.

Under the self-assessment regime you are responsible for submitting your tax return to the Inland Revenue once a year, containing details of all your income including the profits of your self-employed business. The Inland Revenue then have a finite period of time in which to make enquiries into – investigate – your affairs.

If you are to be investigated then the Inspector will write to you and/or your accountant to inform you of this. He or she will demand the presentation of certain documents, set out below, to be delivered by a specific date. Failure to meet that date can result in fines being imposed. Although the Code of Practice asks for taxpayers to be efficient in responding, the question of fines is not mentioned, an unfortunate omission we believe.

The Inspector will demand to see the business records including the books of account, receipts for expenditure and income invoices, the bank statements, paying-in books and cheque books of all business bank accounts. He may ask for non-financial records such as diaries, copies of advertisements placed by the business, and so on. Since there is a requirement in law to maintain these records for at least six years this request is reasonable.

Generally these records are sent to the Inspector's office, but you can ask to have them examined at your business premises.

However, the Inspector may also ask to see personal records of private bank accounts, private building society accounts, dividend receipts, transactions involving the sale or purchase of shares or indeed of any items. There is no requirement to keep such records, but as a taxpayer, and particularly a self-employed one, you will be regarded as guilty unless you can prove yourself otherwise. It is therefore important that when you become self-employed you realize this and maintain your personal records with equal diligence. Vital though this usually is in settling Inland Revenue investigations, you will not find this requirement stated or even recommended in Inland Revenue leaflets and guidelines. The fact of demanding them *is* mentioned in the *Code of Practice 2 – Inland Revenue Investigations'* governing investigations, but by then it may be too late if you have not retained them.

Of more concern under modern legislation is that the Inland Revenue may demand such equally detailed information of your husband, wife, or other relationship-partner. The justification for this is that a 'couple' may hide illegal transactions in the partner's accounts. What is alarming is that the Inland Revenue are well-aware that they have no powers in law to make these demands; individuals must be treated on their own merits. Several years ago we discussed this with an Inspector, who refused to be identified, and who blandly and brusquely stated that if ever he was refused – in his words, if the person being investigated did not volunteer their partner's information – then he would simply commence an investigation into that other person. Put directly to the Inland Revenue they would accept that such an action is improper and not part of their practice. We believe that there are gulfs between the ideals set out in the Inland Revenue's documentation and their actions in practice.

The Inland Revenue's guidelines (*Code of Practice 2 – Inland Revenue Investigations*) indicate that you will be informed of why the investigation has been conducted ('We will always tell you or your accountant the reasons for starting an investigation into your business accounts', *COP2*). This is not true, except in the blandest terms. In fact, the Inland Revenue make a point of not telling you why they believe your accounts or tax return to be in error. Nor will they answer your questions as to why. We recall a case where the Inspector examined the accounts of a language school which had, honestly, shown only modest growth over the years. It got its students from abroad in small numbers and was filled to its own capacity. One of the reasons given for the investigation was that the Inspector had 'noticed an increasing number of students in the university town in which this small, private school was based. It was hardly a sensible basis for the investigation, and in our view probably not the truthful reason.

Furthermore the Inland Revenue state: 'We will start an investigation only if we think that your accounts or Tax Return may not be correct,' (*COP2*). Ironically this may well be true though it should not be. The Inland Revenue have been given powers to make random checks on tax returns but have informally admitted they have no intention of doing so. They will target their enquiries to areas where they feel there are errors. Reading between the lines what has actually happened is that they have sought and obtained powers to legally do what they have in any case been doing for years. They used to have to have a reason for starting an investigation – again, only blandly stated – but now they do not have to have such a reason. They can officially claim it was 'random'. In fact they have stated that they are going to pursue cash businesses and certain other targets.

The implication is chilling. Everyone involved in a cash business is therefore to be assumed guilty of error or fraud. Indeed, every taxpayer under the new regime is to be assumed guilty. After police had been challenged on what were known as the 'suss' laws – it was said they used stop and search in suspicious circumstances as a racist weapon against black people – they were prevented from continuing such searches. Yet those same 'suss' laws are apparently thought appropriate against one targeted sector of society: the self-employed.

Having received your documentation the Inspector will examine it, compiling a case against you in four areas:

- Do the records accurately record your income and expenses so that no income has been omitted and no expenses claimed that should not have been? In other words, are your stated profits correct?

- Can you live from the profits you state you have earned? The Inspector will compile a picture of your personal expenditures and ask you to explain how you paid for your food, home costs, holidays, and so on.
- A capital statement will show the acquisition of your personal wealth and assets over a period. In other words, if you have invested in shares, opened savings accounts, etc. where did you get the money from to do this?
- Sundry information. For example, if you have just taken out a larger mortgage than previously, how did you persuade the lender to give you that mortgage – did you show them higher profits than you are declaring to the Inland Revenue?

The object of this exercise is therefore to determine the true level of profits. The investigation usually examines only one year's accounts but can be extended to other years if serious errors or omissions are uncovered.

Once the Inspector has examined the records, and perhaps corresponded for certain information, in almost all cases he or she will ask for a meeting where you and the Inspector can discuss your business, and the findings to date, face to face. You are not obliged in law to attend such meetings and you can provide the information in documentary form, but a meeting is often the best and quickest way to deal with many of the Inspector's questions.

Such meetings are generally conducted politely and with civility. The Inspector will probe deeply into your private life to determine the facts, and sometimes this can become uncomfortable. But unfortunately there are times when Inspectors use tricks rather than truths. For these and other reasons you are strongly advised to be represented by an accountant. Apart from being experienced in such matters and having been through investigations before he or she will also be able to remain clinical when you are feeling angry; which means that your case is put forward more carefully and appropriately. If you have used an accountant to prepare your accounts then it makes sense in any case for that person to present the figures they are already familiar with. But if you have been going it alone, this is the time to engage an accountant. Bear in mind that if you had been accused of murder you would probably not try to present your own defence in court without legal representation – and, sadly, murderers have a fairer court system on their side. They are deemed to be innocent unless proven guilty; you are assumed guilty from the outset. Do not think of the Inspector of Taxes as the judge; he or she is the prosecution.

You also appear to be up against a political situation. The Inland Revenue believe that if they had the resources to do more enquiries into tax returns and accounts they would be able to generate more tax revenue. It therefore seems to be important to them that as many investigations as possible should result in further tax payments. The small level of 'add-backs', additional tax payable, often vastly outweighs the costs of the investigation borne by the taxpayer. But there is often a high cost in account-ancy fees payable by the person being investigated, to say nothing of the time and work lost in meetings, etc. Sometimes a client will seek to settle an investigation rather than fight it, as the cheaper of two options. It has even been suggested that sometimes the Inland Revenue might pursue investigations, offering settlement in small sums, just to boost their numbers of 'successes', knowing that people will pay up rather than fight. The Revenue have vigorously denied that, but the belief remains widespread in the business community.

An example of the type of situation that gives rise to this belief arose in an investigation handled by us for one of our clients. The client had a turnover of several hundred thousand pounds. After several months of to-ing and fro-ing the Inspector was unable to find fault with any of the figures presented. At a final meeting he resorted to challenging the client for claiming £2 per week towards the cost of heating and lighting in his home for running his office there – a very normal sum, and in fact a very modest claim in his case. In this case, on principle, the client refused to back down stating – and meaning it, we know! – that he would rather go to the Commissioners for an independent ruling regardless of the cost. The Inland Revenue backed away on that occasion.

At the interview the Inland Revenue will make copious notes, a written record of what is discussed. These will then be sent to you and your accountant for your approval. If you believe them to be in error you must challenge them in writing before signing them to confirm your agreement. If you do not they will become the 'true' history of the meeting, whatever the reality. There is no general requirement to sign these records, which was once demanded by the Inspector, but it may still be useful to do so if the matter is likely to go to appeal.

Not all taxpayers are honest. The true number of taxpayers who seek to evade their proper tax liabilities is probably somewhere between the high number suspected by the Inland Revenue and the low numbers that seem evident from accountants' files. But if you, who have just been notified you are under investigation, have anything to hide then this is the time to admit it. Your accountant is also skilled at presenting the facts in the best light.

Before presenting your case it is wise to confirm your own position from the same four viewpoints that the Revenue will use, as noted above. Do not simply focus on sending the Inland Revenue the required records, but think again if the stated profits and other sources of income allow you to have had the lifestyle you have maintained. If not then there could be something amiss in your records and it would be wise to admit that up-front. Unintended errors can get into accounts; better you discover them and volunteer them than they are discovered by the Inspector. Any voluntary disclosures on your part are taken into account in determining the extent of penalties that might later be levied.

It is also best to have a written summary of these four areas with you in the meeting to refer to. In the heat of investigation it is easy to overlook important matters and the Inspector will often not allow correction afterwards unless you have strong evidence to support a revised position. Take any documentary evidence you have to the meeting with the Inspector, and brief your accountant on it in a pre-meeting beforehand. Certainly take any documents that have been requested by the Inspector or you will prolong the investigation, possibly even needing another meeting.

Discuss the position with your spouse or relationship-partner. They may spot something you would overlook. The most common error is to forget the receipt of child benefit (which is non-taxable at the time of writing) which is usually paid directly to the mother's account. This contributes towards household living expenses but if you forget to mention it to the Inspector, you could find yourself paying tax on 'deemed undeclared income' when the gap between your stated profits and your personal expenditures cannot be reconciled. Check also for 'one-off' items that may have contributed: cashing in insurance policies, sale of private assets from the house, gifts from relatives, and so on. All could explain apparently missing money that will otherwise be deemed undeclared income on which you may pay tax, fines and penalties.

The Inland Revenue are, in our experience, respectful of confidentiality. They acknowledge the delicacy of investigations and do not generally release information to friends, relatives, customers or employers unless you have authorized them to do so. *COP2* confirms this, listing the Appeal Commissioners as an example of where information can be given without authorization. This is reasonable, they are more or less the equivalent of a judge in these matters. In one investigation a receipt of £500 was needed to explain income paid into a bank, but the sum had been given by the taxpayer's daughter and son-in-law. Because the son-in-law was a high-profile 'celebrity' the family had not wanted to even give him the worry of telling him that his father-in-law was being investigated. It would have caused great family difficulties between the daughter and son-in-law if the matter had been revealed. But in this case the Inland Revenue were intransigent in demanding confirmation from these third party family members. It took very strong protests from us as the accountants and the Inland Revenue's decision to replace the investigating officer before a sensible compromise was reached. The Inland Revenue satisfied themselves by internally examining the tax records of the son-in-law to show that the gift was within his means. The son-in-law never knew of the matter.

In that investigation it had become apparent that the investigating officer had become somewhat committed to a 'victorious' outcome, and had lost reasonable balance in his enquiries. We were forthright in protesting to the District Inspector, who was extremely helpful. The Inland Revenue did not admit to – or apparently accept – our allegations of lack of proper balance, but, unusually, the officer was removed from the investigation and the matter then quickly resolved by his successor, without any adjustment to our client's stated profits.

The Inland Revenue are obliged to work with accountants or other advisors as stated in their *Code of Practice on Investigations*, and most officers seem to find that easy, and perhaps more professional to handle. There are a few who do not, and taxpayers and accountants sometimes find that Inspectors try to drive a wedge between the client and his or her advisor. In one investigation we dealt with, a client was approached directly by the Inland Revenue and told that his accountants (us) were not co-operating. He knew better and we jointly complained to the District Inspector. She upheld the Inland Revenue's own line and it was four years later, when the matter was resolved entirely to our client's satisfaction, that the Inland Revenue admitted in writing that they had made serious errors of judgement in their handling of the case. They did not specify what errors, and during four years we catalogued a good many. Sexual discrimination certainly seemed to have come into the problem, and we suspected – quite without being able to obtain proof we must add – that racial prejudice had also entered the equation. It is only fair and proper to confirm that once these matters were brought to light and examined by the senior officials we involved that the Inland Revenue were extremely efficient and courteous in bringing matters to an end and apologizing. In fact they finalized the matter very professionally. We will probably never know what the internal consequences were for those involved, and we cannot say more, or name the parties involved, as we still have compensation claims in train at the time of writing.

The Inland Revenue are diligent in providing what information they can, in our experience. When the investigation is started they immediately provide you with leaflets IR72 *Investigations: The Examination of Business Accounts* and IR73 *Inland Revenue Investigations: How Settlements Are Negotiated*, setting out an outline of the investigation and its likely course.

Once you accept that there has been some under-declaration or that you will not be able to disprove the Inspector's allegations, and that therefore additional taxes will have to be paid, it may be sensible to make payments on account as soon as possible to avoid interest charges running on the deemed under-payments.

At the point at which you accept that you will have to pay more tax, for whatever reason, the Inland Revenue have, and will almost certainly exercise, the right to add interest charges and penalties. Interest is, in part, deemed to be a measure of restitution to the Inland Revenue; you have had their money when they should have had it and they could have been earning interest on it so you will have to pay them what they should have earned. You could also have been earning interest on money they would have had, which would not be fair. Interest is calculated at set rates, which can vary according to the economic climate.

Penalties are punishments for your failure to pay the right tax, levied unfortunately whether or not there has been a genuine failure or whether it is just that the Inspector has you trapped between a rock and a hard place (accept the 'add back' or pay more to prove it untrue). There are varying degrees of penalty depending on circumstances. Finalizing the investigation also involves signing a declaration, a Certificate of Disclosure, that you have now given details of everything that should be disclosed. The Inland Revenue state that they do not 'start another investigation in the future simply because something was wrong on a previous occasion' (*COP2*), and mostly we have found this to be true but we have known of rare situations where people have been investigated immediately after a previous investigation for no obvious proper reason we could identify.

There are levels of complaint you can make if you believe your investigation is not being conducted reasonably. There is an Officer in Charge at the Inland Revenue district dealing with you who can look into the matter. We believe that where prejudicial attitudes arise in individual inspectors this level of complaint usually resolves the matter fairly. You may, if that does not bring a resolution, also apply to an Inland Revenue Controller who deals with the section of the Inland Revenue that covers your area.

The question of appeals procedure we shall shortly also examine.

There is also an Adjudicator, who examines complaints against the Inland Revenue (and the Contributions Agency and the Customs and Excise). At the time of writing the present Adjudicator, Elizabeth Filkin, has made herself very high-profile, reflecting it seems an obvious wish to be approached and approachable. Our enquiries with accountants suggest that she is seen to be very genuinely concerned to perform her role fairly. However, the Adjudicator is limited to dealing with the way in which the Inland Revenue have dealt with taxpayers, not with the facts of investigations. The Adjudicator can examine complaints of excessive delay in dealing with your affairs, of errors in the way they have been approached, of discourtesy and of any perceived lack of fairness in discretionary matters. The Adjudicator does not hear appeals. The adjudicator may only examine complaints based on matters arising after 5 April 1993, and should normally be approached as quickly as possible after a need is perceived. Generally, you would be expected to have complained within six months of the matter about which you were displeased.

It is also possible to complain to the Ombudsman, an independent Parliamentary Commissioner. The Ombudsman can look at complaints the Adjudicator has examined, but not vice versa. He can only investigate complaints made through a Member of Parliament.

Once the Inspector has all three components in place: tax deemed lost, interest and penalties, then he or she will ask you to agree with him or her and 'make an offer' in settlement. If the offer covers the amounts he or she believes reasonable then it will be accepted and when paid that is the end of the matter.

If agreement cannot be made between the taxpayer and the Revenue then the matter can go to an independent appeal procedure. It is generally a fair procedure, and indeed one that the Inland Revenue often seek to avoid because it often goes 'against them'. But in order to 'dissuade' you from using the procedure there is a threat to be wary of. Simply, the Inspector sets out a level of penalty which may be mitigated for various reasons stated above, and expects your obedience to that figure. If you do not 'make an offer' in that same vein and the matter has to go to appeal then the mitigation is removed and the Inspector will demand full penalties. The Inland Revenue put it thus: 'The figures we put forward may have to be higher than those we suggested to you during our negotiations, as they might have been "without prejudice", and the Commissioners will need to consider all the facts and issues which you and we believe to be relevant,' (*COP2*). In other words, there is a price to pay if you wish to defend yourself.

Assuming that you do choose to go to the Commissioners then another leaflet which is not usually provided unless asked for is IR37 *Appeals Against Tax* which sets out the appeals procedure and describes the role of the independent Commissioners. But this leaflet hardly prepares you for what is to follow. Up until this point there has been the semblance of co-operation between you and the Inspector. Frankly, at this point from the Inspector's point of view, the gloves come off and you recognize an aggressive prosecution for what it actually has been all along. The Inland

Revenue state that 'Asking for this [appeal] to happen will not be regarded as a lack of co-operation on your part . . .' (*COP2*). However, some inspectors respond as if they do feel it is a lack of co-operation.

In fact from any point during the investigation you have had the right to go to appeal, but this rarely happens unless there is a deadlock in trying to find an agreement, with neither party willing to back down from their position.

Once that deadlock is recognized then the Inspector will simply raise an assessment – a demand for money – based on his or her view of the position. You then have 30 days to appeal against it, and the appeal is set before the Commissioners.

It is a very formal procedure. Both sides present their case, and exchange details of their case to each other beforehand, and the Commissioners determine the case on the basis of the facts presented. Witnesses may be called and formal statements presented. You should be represented by at least someone who can present your case well (though it does not have to be a professionally qualified person), probably your accountant, and almost certainly a solicitor. The Inland Revenue field very aggressive solicitors for their side.

The Adjudicator

We mentioned above the Adjudicator, who examines the conduct of the Inland Revenue. It is worth looking at the procedures that will likely be followed if you decide to make a complaint to her office.

Apart from giving 'routine' matters such as details of yourself and your complaint it is suggested that you also set out what rectification you require. Is it compensation? Is it an apology? Or both? Or something else?

You should set out any costs that you feel you have wrongly incurred as the Adjudicator can recommend compensation payments. If the Adjudicator can resolve matters between you and the Inland Revenue she will endeavour to do so. If not then she will make a recommendation for resolution. The Inland Revenue have agreed to be bound by her recommendations except in special circumstances which would then be brought to attention in her published annual report. In such circumstances you would not be identified.

The future of investigations

Considering that the process of investigation, while absolutely necessary, can be unfair and unfairly administered, the future for the self-employed looks bleak indeed.

For many reasons the Inland Revenue intends to step up their investigation processes, raining down on many more taxpayers than ever before. Considering that they seem to exhibit a bias towards employment and the PAYE system and a corresponding bias against self-employment, then it could be argued that this concentration might frighten people away from self-employment where there is choice and that the Inland Revenue might see this as an advantage. True or not, the Inland Revenue's stated belief is that they can capture more tax if they do more investigations.

Self-assessment was a necessary step towards that end. By placing the onus and the practical work of tax compliance on the taxpayers they freed up money and personnel to enable them to conduct more in-depth examinations.

They have made it quite clear that in the first year or so of self-assessment to the time of writing they had hardly begun using their new powers, and that they intend to do so much more in the future than ever before.

Other 'taxing' investigations

Nor is the Inland Revenue the only body that can undertake rigorous scrutiny of your records. Such investigations can be applied by the VAT office and the Department of Social Security. Specialist areas can also include Health and Safety Examinations including those covering Fire Regulations, and Data Protection Regulations for computer users. Specialist industries have their own regulating or overseeing bodies; ABTA for travel agents, SFA for the financial services sector, the Ministry of Agriculture, Fisheries and Foods for farming, CORGI for gas fitters, and so on. Trade journals and industry-specific publications and promotional events will supply information relating to your specific industry regarding these bodies.

The future . . . the more frightening speculations

There is an attitude afoot in the current government which while not yet affecting the self-employed directly, can hardly fail to hit them in the end. The 11 October 1998 issue of the *Sunday Times* reported on General Anti-Avoidance Rules (GAAR), a consultative document that had just been issued by the Chancellor which – whatever any eventual laws might be framed like – gives an indication of his thinking. Basically, there has always been a division between tax evasion – not paying properly due taxes, which is illegal – and tax avoidance, which is arranging your affairs to minimize your tax bills and which has always been perfectly sensible and legal. GAAR, originally due to be implemented in April 2000, is currently on hold but likely to be implemented in the future, as indicated in the 1999 budget. It would give the power to the Inland Revenue to ignore any transaction that it did not like if it thought that without it more tax might be gained. No taxpayer would ever be able to plan his or her taxes, because it would be enshrined in law that the goalposts could 'legitimately' be moved by the Inland Revenue after the fact – after they had had a chance to see if they liked the way you used the law as it existed. As a way of bringing in the system without raising too much protest – governments are probably still wary of the Poll Tax rebellions that eventually contributed to the downfall of Margaret Thatcher – the plan is to target big corporations first. But reaching down to the self-employed individuals is surely only a natural extension of such an attitude.

Not yet even being mentioned within the framework of taxation at all – but certainly open to that area – is a chilling proposal by the government to seize the assets of people suspected, but not convicted, of crime. As outlined in the *Daily Mail* of 11 November 1998, 'new laws will allow police to confiscate the assets of suspected major criminals even if they have not yet been convicted of any offence'. The article went on to say, 'At present only drug money can be confiscated ... [but] ... the new legislation will apply to the proceeds of any crime. . . . Officers will simply have to show that someone living in luxury ... cannot prove his assets were amassed legally.' Already, as this book has shown, the Inland Revenue have powers to 'make up' assumed undeclared incomes and then tax them unless the accused can prove his or her innocence. Why not an extension to simply confiscating the assets of those the Inland Revenue have made up figures for, without having to bother with the inconvenience of court procedures? And just as in the GAAR point raised above, the government does not intend to frighten off individuals too early, claiming that only 'major criminals' will be targeted. But once a precedent has been set, are the small businessmen and women in this country not a potential target?

Of course there would be limits and guidelines to both the above legislations, but some very fundamental civil liberties would surely have been breached. And once a breach appears in the dam, a flood usually follows.

20
Red Alert

As we have said earlier, unfortunately for the owners, nearly 90 per cent of all new businesses fail within a five-year period, and whatever the underlying reasons are for the business failure, the symptoms are basically the same: the business runs out of cash and/or its ability to obtain more.

In general discussions with people whose businesses did just that it is apparent that they saw the problems coming but chose to ignore them on the grounds that next month something would turn up. Going self-employed is an optimistic journey and this very optimism can often be the lever that topples people over the financial cliff. In this chapter we are concerned with the warning signals that tell us that a business is heading towards problems, how we read them and what corrective action can be taken. Basically we can divide the warning signals into two groups, personal and business, although we fully appreciate that the two are intertwined: personal problems may effect the running of the business and the business problems may impact upon your personal life.

Personal issues

Divorce
The break-up of a relationship is not only emotionally taxing but is usually very costly. Time that should be spent on running the business is now spent on sorting out private affairs. It may be necessary to re-finance the business to pay off the other partner, or houses may have to be sold or re-mortgaged to raise new capital.

Losing your nerve

People do lose their nerve in business and the warning signals are both complex and subtle. Symptoms include not wishing to grow the business both in terms of assets and people. This is demonstrated by a refusal to take on more business, and not expanding new and existing product lines or services. The owner will often fall into the activity trap, i.e. getting bogged down in day-to-day trivia and details that do not add value to the business.

Age and health

Running your own business needs energy and application as well as determination. Too many self-employed business people continue working well past their personal sell-by dates, often to the detriment of their health and the health of the business. Age and health also affects the work ethic and temperament of the owner which in turn can have an adverse effect upon customers.

Boredom

Boredom is not restricted to the so-called employed wage slaves. Self-employed people do get bored and often very quickly. This state of mind usually leads to two alternatives: the entrepreneurial instinct to do something else or defeatism which means plodding away at work that is no longer interesting, and in consequence the business may never realize its full potential.

The paradox of wealth

There may well come a stage in the life of the business when the owner has fulfilled the ambitions set, particularly in terms of assets and other wealth. Paradoxically at this point because the owner is no longer hungry this often leads to the running down of the business and the loss of wealth built up.

The denial of the personal warning signs are often a major contributor to business failure. The secret is to acknowledge and face up to the impending problems immediately and take necessary corrective action. If you are having to re-finance the business, talk and be open to your bank manager. Recognize when you have lost interest in the business, and realize when age and ill health are limiting your ability to run it. Consider the options open to you, e.g. sell it as a going concern, or recruit a more confident, hungry and market aggressive person as a possible partner who will buy out your interest over a sensible period of time.

Business issues

Cashflow

Money is the life blood of a business and as we have already said the majority of companies fail because they run out of cash. The issues to consider are why and how this can be avoided. There is usually no one reason why businesses run out of cash, but most are due to poor management decisions. We have interviewed many self-employed people who have lost their businesses and below is a summary of the mistakes they made:

- A decline in sales not matched by a reduction in outgoings, resulting in declining profit margins.
- A psychological barrier to admitting that the company is bleeding cash.
- Bad debts. There is a tendency for small companies to trade with a few large customers, and if a large customer goes broke it can bring smaller companies down with it.
- Spending cash on assets such as buildings, machinery, vehicles, etc. and not keeping enough back to pay operating expenses, e.g. rent, wages, materials, etc.
- Owners taking too much money out of the business by way of inflated salaries, pensions, cars and other benefits.
- Employing too many people and being unwilling to let them go when sales are down.
- Tying up too much money in stocks that are unnecessary to service the current level of sales.
- Borrowing too much money from banks and other lenders so that the interest payable becomes unserviceable. Especially true when interest rates go up.
- Spending money on new product and service developments that do not get off the ground.
- Expanding the business when the market is stagnant or contracting.
- Spending too much money on expensive offices and equipment before the business has generated enough cash.
- Losing control of running expenses.

- Banks reducing overdraft facilities and/or loans, or indeed calling in the loans.
- Lack of financial planning and control so that the owners were unaware that they were running out of cash.
- Large-scale financial theft.

Cashflow management is an essential tool in financially managing your business. It is not difficult but does require planning and regular monitoring. The following ten point action plan is recommended.

1. At least every six months draw up a detailed cashflow model showing for each month the expected income from all sources and expenditure. Monthly compare the actual results with your forecast and investigate the variances. Update your model on each occasion that new information is received, e.g. winning a new customer or an increase in a major cost item.
2. If you expect sales to take a downturn, then reduce your expenditure immediately by the appropriate percentage.
3. Control your costs, run the business mean and lean.
4. Never spend money on 'nice to have' unnecessary assets.
5. Consider hire purchase and leasing as an alternative to using scarce cash to purchase your essential assets.
6. Keep staffing to a minimum, and use temporary or contract staff for busy periods.
7. Only draw out from the company money that it can afford. Paying yourself wages from an overdraft is a fool's paradise.
8. Keep stocks to the absolute minimum.
9. Spread your borrowings, i.e. overdrafts, medium-term loans, hire purchase, leasing, credit cards, etc., over different institutions so as to avoid all your commitments being reduced or called in at one point in time.
10. Keep your bank fully informed of your cashflow requirements and if necessary furnish them with monthly/quarterly financial information.

Financial tools and measures
Nearly all businesses are at some time subject to business cycles and even the best run companies will occasionally run short of cash. The purpose of bank overdrafts is to finance these short-

term cash situations. However, there are financial tools and measures that the self-employed business person may wish to take as an alternative to, or in conjunction with, bank facilities:

- Reduce your stock holdings and convert excess stocks into cash. For retailers this may well include holding a sale or special promotions.
- Delay paying your creditors and come to an arrangement with your major creditors for payments on account over this lean period. Negotiate longer credit terms with your suppliers.
- Put a moratorium on all expenditure including hiring of staff, overtime, etc.
- Sell any surplus assets you can but do not be tempted into a fire sale.
- If possible reduce your drawings from the business.

Above all keep your bank and creditors informed of what you are doing, in order to protect your credit rating and business reputation.

Gross profit margin

It is important to closely monitor the performance of your business and a useful calculation is the gross profit margin which is computed as follows:

sales minus cost of sales (e.g. raw materials) = gross profit

This can be expressed as a percentage:

$$\frac{\text{gross profit}}{\text{sales income}} \times 100$$

Any change in the gross profit percentage that is not planned is a warning signal that the cost of sales has changed. If the gross profit margin increases you can either keep the extra profit or reduce your sales price in order, for example, to attract new customers and increase your market share. Any increase in your cost of sales means that you must either accept a lower profit, increase the selling price or try and source the raw materials more cheaply.

Net profit margin

As important is the net profit margin which is calculated as follows:

sales minus total expenditure = net profit

Again this can be expressed as a percentage:

$$\frac{\text{net profit}}{\text{sales income}} \times 100$$

Assuming that the gross profit percentage is constant then any change to the net profit percentage needs investigation. Obviously an increase in net profit means that the costs are down, although it could mean that you have not accounted for some expenditure. If the net profit decreases it probably means that costs have increased and it is useful to pinpoint which and why so that corrective action is taken.

We strongly recommend that you do the above calculations monthly.

Customer count

For retail shops, fast food outlets, book shops, restaurants, etc. it is a very useful exercise to keep a log of the number of people visiting your premises, and certainly for retailers to divide the count into purchasers and browsers. An upward trend speaks for itself, i.e. you are getting it right; a downward trend needs looking into and should be treated as a flashing warning signal. Examples of reasons for a decline in customers may include some of the following:

- *Competition opened next door.* In this case visit the competition and compare the prices, product range and service with your own.
- *The superstore effect.* Difficult to compete with on prices, however, you can compete on service and building customer relationships.
- *Not stocking the right products.* Keep detailed stock turn records and take into account people's changing buying habits as published in the press and in particular trade journals.

- *Monitor population age change profiles*. Perhaps there is little point in opening a kids' outfitters in, say, Worthing, Sussex, where the majority of the population is over 40.
- *Closure of major employers*. Consider the plight of self-employed business people in the UK's mining and steel towns over the past decades.
- *Bad customer service*. Slow staff, staff not understanding the products and rude staff are sure to lose you customers.
- *Location, location, location*. The retail experts tell us that location is of the utmost importance. A dwindling customer base may mean that you are now trading from the wrong place.
- *Customer lifestyle changes*. Customers follow trends and are very fickle in their tastes. The problem of being in the popular trend business is that you have to keep identifying new ones.

The downward slope

In the unfortunate event that your business does get into financial difficulties you will need advice and to take action to protect your assets. From our experience most self-employed business people are fully aware when their business is in trouble but often try to hang on out of a false sense of pride, or loyalty to customers, creditors and staff. However, in the event that you realize that it is not possible to trade out of difficulties the following course of action is recommended:

- Talk to your bank manager. Explain in detail the position and have all the relevant financial information available.
- If the underlying business is sound but the initial and continuing debt is the problem, explore the options open to you, e.g. sale of the business, bringing in a partner with capital, or a total re-financing package.
- Take advice from a qualified accountant who specializes in liquidations and receiverships, as well as arrangements with creditors.
- If you know you are trading at a loss do not enter into any financial or other business commitments as you will now be potentially liable on a personal basis for debts arising.
- Do not borrow any more money from the bank or other lenders.

- Do not pledge or mortgage any of your personal assets, e.g. house, for short-term business debt.

But do not let this high failure rate, and these red alert signs, frighten you off. The authors' combined business experience of over 50 years in all fields of industry and commerce shows that while businesses may fail, people survive. And most go on to new businesses and take their experiences – positive and negative – with them and thereby increase their chances of later success.

Enjoy your enterprise – and good luck!

Useful Addresses

The authors

John Spencer and Adrian Pruss
The Leys
2c Leyton Road
Harpenden
Herts AL5 2TL

Telephone: (01582) 468592
Fax: (01582) 461979
e-mail: jspencer@dial.pipex.com

Accountancy

The Institute of Chartered
Accountants in England and
Wales
Chartered Accountants' Hall
PO Box 433
Moorgate Place
London EC2P 2BJ

Telephone: (0171) 920 8100

Franchising

British Franchise Association
Thames View
Newton Road
Henley-on-Thames
Oxon RG9 1HG

Telephone: (01491) 578050
Fax: (01491) 573517

Grants and support

The Department of Trade and
Industry
1 Victoria Street
London SW1H 0ET

Telephone: (0171) 215 5000

Health and Safety

Health and Safety Executive
Information Centre
Broad Lane
Sheffield S3 7HQ

Telephone: (0541) 545500

Insurances and pensions

Association of British Insurers
51 Gresham Street
London EC2V 7HG

Telephone: (0171) 600 3333
Fax: (0171) 696 8999

Insurance Ombudsman
City Gate
135 Park Street
London SE1 9EA

Telephone: (0171) 928 4488

Interviewees' organizations

Martin Attridge is the principal of Development by Design
4 Meadway
Harpenden
Herts AL5 1JL
Telephone: (01582) 460440

Onay Faiz of Phoenix Training Network – management training services
Studio House
168 Manor Road
Cogges
Witney
Oxon OX8 6SS
Telephone: (01993) 852494
Fax: (01993) 852465

Maynard Leigh Associates are a training, consultancy and coaching organization whose clients include many of the largest companies in the UK and abroad
Marvic House
Bishops Road
London SW6 7AD
Telephone: (0171) 385 2588
Fax: (0171) 381 4110

Bob Rontaler is MD of a company trading in the amber market
Goldmajor Ltd
Derwent House
Arden Road
London W13 8RN
Telephone: (0181) 579 0588

B. Howard Thompson
Human Resources Consultant
3 Shaftesbury House
Trinity Street
London SE1 4JF
Telephone: (0171) 357 9189
Fax: (0171) 403 6803

James Wildman of Wild Communications – editorial, marketing and PR, print and design services for clients promoting their businesses
Parlour Studios
Buckland Road
Bampton
Oxon OX18 2AA
Telephone: (01993) 850705 / 852494
Fax: (01993) 850545 / 852465

Gerry Zierler is MD of Zierler Media
19 Greenwood Place
Kentish Town
London NW5 1LB
Telephone: (0171) 284 2848

Index